Border Crossings

AMERICAN INTERACTIONS

WITH ISRAELIS

Lucy Shahar and David Kurz

The InterAct Series

GEORGE W. RENWICK, Series Editor

Other books in the series:

Border Crossings
AMERICAN INTERACTIONS
WITH ISRAELIS

Lucy Shahar and David Kurz

INTERCULTURAL PRESS, INC.

First published by Intercultural Press. For information, contact:

Intercultural Press, Inc.   Nicholas Brealey Publishing
PO Box 700   36 John Street
Yarmouth, Maine 04096, USA   London, WC1N 2AT, UK
001-207-846-5168   44-207-430-0224
Fax: 001-207-846-5181   Fax: 44-207-404-8311
www.interculturalpress.com   www.nbrealey-books.com

Book design and production: Patty J. Topel
Cover design: Lois Leonard Stock

Printed in the United States of America

05   04   03   02   01   3   4   5   6   7

Library of Congress Cataloging-in-Publication Data

Shahar, Lucy.
   Border crossings : American interactions with Israelis /
Lucy Shahar and David Kurz.
      p.   cm. — (InterAct series)
   Includes bibliographical references.
   ISBN 1-877864-31-5 (pbk.)
   1. National characteristics, Israeli. 2. National characteris-
tics, American. 3. Business travel—Israel. 4. Israel-Foreign
public opinion, American. 5. Public opinion—United States.
I. Kurz, David. II. Title. III. Series.
DS113.3.S52   1995
303.48'27305694—dc20   95-6136
                                CIP

Table of Contents

Acknowledgments

Our special thanks to all the American and Israeli workshop participants whose comments and observations served as a basis for many of the critical incidents. We're indebted to Dorothy Kushner for the idea of the coloring book, to Cindy Rahav for suggesting a title that tied everything together, to Chen Gratz Shmueli for her assistance on Appendix B, and to David Kreizelman for his advice on Part II. We appreciate the support and professionalism of our editors, David and Kathleen Hoopes and Toby Frank. We are, of course, grateful to our families and friends for their contributions, encouragement and, especially, their patience.

Authors' Note

Although it may seem presumptuous, two Americans who have immigrated to Israel have undertaken the task of explaining Israeli culture. But that is not so strange. Often the underlying components of a culture are clearer to people who have grown up outside it than to those who are native born.

Twenty-odd years of living in Israel—undergoing the adjustment process, becoming part of an Israeli family, sending a son to the army (Lucy), being a soldier (David), gradually feeling that we belong—have enabled us to develop a personal perspective on Israeli culture. Fifteen years of conducting cross-cultural workshops for Israelis and Americans (Lucy) and fifteen years of community development work with immigrant groups (David) have given us an opportunity to understand how Americans and Israelis perceive and misperceive each other. Over the years we have developed and experimented with many strategies for dealing with American-Israeli cultural differences. The results are summarized in this book.

As we complete our writing, enormous changes are taking place in the Middle East. Formerly implacable enemies have exchanged handshakes, first on the White House lawn and later in the Middle East itself.

What does it all mean? None of us really knows. Those of us who live in the Middle East are not at a simple crossroads. We're standing at a multilevel, multidirectional intersection. The road signs aren't clear. Neither is the speed limit.

If and when peace comes, will it bring changes in Israeli culture? Perhaps. We can speculate about what may happen in the distant future. However, we know from history that it takes years, often generations, for significant changes to occur in a people's set of behaviors, norms, and attitudes. In the foreseeable future, Israelis will continue to reflect the traits described in this book, and American interactions with Israelis will maintain the form outlined in the following chapters.

There's more. We've yet to experience a general peace in the region, but there is an abundance of new opportunities. The Middle East will increasingly be open to business, tourism, and diplomatic activity—with Israel an integral part of a regional network. An understanding of the cultural context of American-Israeli interactions seems more important than ever.

Lucy Shahar, Tel Aviv
David Kurz, Jerusalem

Introduction

Welcome to the Middle East. Or is it the Middle East? If you arrive in Israel from other parts of the region, you will certainly get the impression that you are in a Western country. To begin with, so many people look "out of place," European rather than Middle Eastern. The youngsters, of course, are wearing the nearly universal jeans, sneakers, and T-shirts. That doesn't surprise you. The adults do; they may be fair or dark, but their appearance is also almost universally Western. Although they may dress more casually than their European or American counterparts, their Lacoste shirts, Levis, and Reeboks, their minis, tights, and "granny boots" make it difficult for you to distinguish the "natives" from the tourists. You walk into a supermarket. The layout, the packaging, the computerized scanner at the checkout counter are recognizably Western. Outside, you see people waiting in line at an automated bank teller.

You leave the supermarket and walk five blocks to the *shuk*, or open-air market. Suddenly, you are in the Middle East as you know or imagined it. Shouting. Bargaining. Dead chickens hanging in the open air. Lots of physical contact. Noise. Dirt. "Local color." The music you hear sounds Oriental. It is unfamiliar, strange. The food on sale at the stalls is

Middle Eastern—hummos, felafel, pita. It looks and tastes like the food you ate in Cairo or in a Middle Eastern restaurant in the States. You see a veritable "salad" of faces—white, tan, black, brown—and a full range of body exposure—from women in tank tops and bare-chested men in shorts to the thoroughly clothed ultrareligious. You hear Hebrew, Arabic, and many other languages you can't identify.

Supermarket/shuk. Brash/modest. Clean and orderly/dirty and noisy. If you think that you are getting mixed messages, you're right. Israel is both Western and Eastern, secular and religious. Expect to be confused. While sharp contrasts exist in all Middle Eastern countries, they are especially marked in Israel. Much of Israel is truly Western and is becoming more so at a "future shock" pace. Westernization is not simply a facade or a phenomenon confined to metropolitan locales or the economic and political elite. Supermarkets, shopping centers, and automated bank tellers exist in the most remote areas. They are taken for granted as part of the Israeli lifestyle, as are freeways, MTV, CNN, fast-food outlets, and cellular phones.

On the other hand, perhaps the country is not so Western after all. When you enter the shopping mall (Western), the behavior and ambience which you encounter are Middle Eastern: that's the surprise. Much of the sense of the Middle East that you found in the shuk is replicated in the mall: high noise level, physical closeness and contact, a sense of messiness and crowding—some of the shuk has been brought inside.

Israel is undergoing an economic and cultural transition. Western technology, free market behavior, and liberal social norms are percolating down and subtly changing both the old Middle Eastern patterns and those established by the Eastern European socialists who founded Israeli society. What is being created is a constantly changing blend of East and West. The image of the Bedouin trailed by several veiled women taking money out of an automated bank teller and entering a shopping mall is not farfetched. It is into this strange kaleidoscope that you are now venturing.

Our goal is to provide you with a conceptual understanding of Israeli culture and a repertoire of strategies for dealing with American-Israeli cultural differences. We will serve as cultural translators, interpreting local norms and behavior patterns. As we report on the cultural landscape, we will bring elements of the Israeli character into sharper focus. Our challenge is to identify those elements without reducing them to oversimplifications or stereotypes.

When people speak about Israeli culture, they are usually referring to that of the Jewish majority. Arabs comprise about 16 percent of Israel's population. Politically and culturally, they are a significant minority within the Jewish state. For the most part, however, our book focuses on the Jewish majority whose culture is that which most sojourners encounter.

After a broad look at Israeli culture in general, we will be concentrating, quite frankly, on your counterparts—those Israelis involved on a more or less regular basis with the Western, primarily English-speaking, world. They will most likely be professionals—in business, government, academia, philanthropic organizations, the diplomatic community, or the military. Their behavior and the cultural and social forces which have shaped it provide the raw material for this book and serve as the source of the examples we use. Others— waiters, clerks, and bureaucrats—will also figure in our case studies. After all, they will be prominent among the cast of players in your daily interactions. You will also be a player; in fact, there are times when you will be convinced that you have suddenly been cast in a theater of the absurd.

We deliberately place our discussion of Israeli culture in a broader historical and social context. Part I sets the stage. Israel is an immigrant society with ethnic and national communities from all over the world. We briefly describe what happened in the process of amalgamation and how it has affected the present.

Is Israel a melting pot? A pressure cooker? A salad bowl? Are there common denominators, patterns which the newcomer can decipher? Israel is both a puzzle and a challenge. What are the questions most newcomers ask, and how can they be answered? These are the subjects of chapters 1-3.

In chapter 4, we discuss the behaviors and attitudes which we believe are recognizably Israeli. Using three visual images, we identify nine specific cultural characteristics and explore how they are expressed in various settings. Much of the discussion revolves around the issue of borders. We use a picture in a child's coloring book to reinforce this point. Borders, or boundaries, are generally ill defined in Israeli social, commercial, and professional relationships, and Israeli society is extraordinarily informal. Lines of authority are blurred, job descriptions and professional territories are loosely defined, and the boundaries between personal and professional, private and public are unclear. Social norms include very few do's and don'ts.

Because borders tend to be fuzzy, border crossings—perceived by Americans as challenges to authority or violations of personal space—are easy for Israelis. Some borders, of course, are clearly defined in Israel. There *are* rules and regulations. But Israelis prefer not to stay within designated boundaries, even when they are clearly defined. Spontaneity, individualism, the impulse to test the limits, indeed, to challenge the rules, simply don't allow for a very tidy picture in the coloring book. In fact, we've chosen *Border Crossings* as the title of the book because it seems to be the single most appropriate metaphor for Israeli behavior and cultural norms. And differences in American and Israeli attitudes toward borders, as well as the perception of borders as clear or fuzzy, explain many of the misunderstandings that occur in interactions between the two groups. Americans seem to experience difficulty dealing with Israel's cultural ambiguities and fuzzy social and professional boundaries.

The term "recognizably Israeli characteristics" requires a

disclaimer. When it comes to attitudes and behaviors in any culture, we can, at best, refer to *tendencies*, that is, those behaviors and attitudes that the culture encourages or discourages. Otherwise, we run the risk of being trapped in rigid stereotypes.

It may seem as though we mention scores of Israeli cultural traits. In fact, our discussion revolves around our choice of nine characteristics that repeat themselves in various settings. They are:

informal patterns of personal interaction
spontaneity
improvisational approach to problem solving
self-confidence
positive attitude toward risk taking
direct communication style
group orientation coexisting with strong individualism
readiness to question authority
casual attitude toward rules and regulations

Israeli culture is similar to American culture in many ways, but there are subtle and sometimes not so subtle differences which distinguish one from the other. Some of the characteristics listed above, e.g., informality, are also descriptive of American society. In Israel, they either exist to a greater degree, express themselves differently, or are defined differently. We begin an exploration of those subtleties in Part II.

One approach to cultural differences is to examine mutual perceptions. Israelis view their behavior one way. Americans see that same behavior and label it differently. The reverse, of course, is also true. Our chart, "Same Behavior/Separate Labels: The Differences at a Glance," presents those mutual perceptions in table form, and serves as a handy reference point. The next chapters expand upon this framework and describe how the structure developed, how it functions today, and how you can best use this information.

In a series of critical incidents—case studies based on real situations—we juxtapose Israelis and Americans attempting to communicate across cultural barriers. The difficulties they encounter are those which you, the reader, may also encounter. We offer a systematic analysis of American-Israeli cultural differences as they appear in the incidents. Chapters 5, 6, 7, and 8 deal with cultural differences in commercial, bureaucratic, professional, and social settings.

Each of us reacts to similar stimuli in different ways. There is no one correct way to adjust or respond to another culture. Some people become depressed over a particular encounter; others become exhilarated. Some choose to withdraw; others explode. Although there are difficulties, there are also strategies which can be used to overcome them. We suggest a few. Throughout the book, we encourage you to think about choices, and we try to offer several options.

In two appendices, we present and review a more detailed menu of coping strategies. Exploring benefits and costs, we encourage you to experiment in order to discover the strategies that are effective, appropriate, and consistent with your personal style. Everybody has his or her "this far and no further" line. We invite you to stretch, and to feel okay about the limits to your stretching.

You may be a novice or an old-timer when it comes to American-Israeli encounters. You may be a visitor to Israel, or someone who has never set foot in the country but is nevertheless engaged in ongoing contacts with Israeli colleagues or friends. It doesn't matter. At some point in your reading we hope that you will sense the "Yeah!" or "Aha!" that signals things are beginning to fall into place.

"Yaaala, chevre, kadima!" (*Rough translation: "Enough talk, action!"*)

Part I

Setting the Scene

Israeli Culture as a
Puzzle and a Challenge

Describing Israeli culture presents a formidable challenge. Indeed, there are skeptics who doubt that a single Israeli culture or *the* Israeli character even exist. They see a pile of pieces to a jigsaw puzzle and believe that it is impossible to put them together into a cohesive picture.

Israel is, of course, a heterogeneous society, as are the United States and all societies composed largely of immigrant groups. There are many ethnic communities existing side by side, ingredients for a melting pot that haven't completely melted and probably never will; there are those who believe that they never should. However, there are elements which lend cohesion and produce a common frame of reference.

We propose to examine the key pieces of the jigsaw puzzle in order to show that, as disparate as they are, they do, in fact, fit together.

Israel is a nation founded by and for Jews consciously experimenting with the creation of a society based on Jewish ethics, Jewish traditions, and a Jewish political ideology called Zionism. Its society and institutions were founded by immigrants from Europe though a sizable proportion of the population—Jewish and non-Jewish alike—comes from the Middle

3

East or North Africa. It has few natural resources. Conventional wisdom places the country among developing nations. Yet its high-tech, export-oriented economy is one of the fastest growing in the world, and Israel is in the process of becoming a regional economic and financial center. The aspirations of its citizens, as well as the medical care they receive and their longevity and educational levels, resemble those in affluent Western societies. Israel is a country of stark social and cultural contrasts. Continuous and rapid change is the rule rather than the exception.

Much has been written about these issues, all of which is essential to our understanding of the Israeli mindset and the cultural context in which Israelis live. We will not be able to explore all of them in depth here, but we will touch on many of them in order to identify the unique impact they have on the people with whom you are likely to come in contact.

At a later point in the chapter, we will discuss the significance of terms like "melting pot" and "salad bowl," both of which are used to describe immigrant societies. And throughout the chapter, we will employ a variety of other metaphors, e.g., jigsaw puzzle, mosaic, pressure cooker. Our goal is to exploit the image that each metaphor evokes in order to bring into focus various facets of Israeli culture.

At this juncture, we'll focus on the ingredients in the immigrant mixture that is Israel. Who lives here now? What is "here"? When and why did various groups arrive in the area? When it comes to Israel, even these relatively simple questions become complicated indeed.

A Middle Eastern Piece of Real Estate

During the twentieth century, the piece of real estate known today as Israel has had three owners. From 1517 until 1917, it was one of the provinces of the Ottoman Empire. The British took control in 1918, after the First World War. In

1922, they were entrusted with the League of Nations Mandate for Palestine, which included the territory of present-day Israel and the Kingdom of Jordan. The British Mandate in the part west of the Jordan River ended on May 14, 1948. On the same day, the State of Israel was proclaimed and the Israeli War of Independence officially began. The war made the new state a reality but did not settle the question of Israel's borders.

For thirty-one years (1948-79), all the border demarcations on the map of Israel were cease-fire or armistice lines left over from the War of Independence and other wars that followed: the 1967 Six-Day War and the 1973 Yom Kippur War. In 1979, the Camp David Agreement with Egypt established the only mutually agreed upon border between Israel and an Arab state. (The Taba arbitration decision in 1989 settled a border dispute with Egypt left unresolved in the 1979 agreement.) There is as yet no peace treaty with Lebanon, but the border is not contested. In October, 1994, Israel and Jordan signed a comprehensive peace treaty establishing an internationally recognized border between the two countries.

Despite other recent dramatic developments—the signing of the 1993 Oslo Accords with the Palestine Liberation Organization (PLO), and the beginning of negotiations with Syria—the borders between Israel and these neighbors have yet to be agreed upon. The future of the Golan Heights rests upon the outcome of negotiations with Syria. The final status, including borders, of the West Bank and the Gaza Strip depend upon the outcome of negotiations with the PLO.

In other words, as of the publication of this book, Israel still lacks a clear geographic identity. Critical segments of its borders are fuzzy, though the situation is becoming less ambiguous. (In the Middle East, one has to learn to live with varying degrees of ambiguity.)

The Demographic Mosaic

Who lives in Israel today? Various waves of immigration have produced a demographic mosaic: Jews constitute approximately 82 percent of a total population of 5.4 million. Over half are native born. (Native-born Israelis are known as *sabras*. A Hebrew word, "sabra" is a cactus fruit which is tough and prickly on the outside, soft and sweet on the inside. Israelis believe the character of those born in the country is similar to the sabra.) Others come from eighty countries of origin, speak more than thirty languages, and follow a wide variety of Jewish religious and ethnic traditions.

Arabs comprise about 16 percent of the total population. They are primarily Muslim, although there is a sizable Christian community. The overwhelming majority of Israeli Arabs are Palestinian. Bedouins, a minority within the Arab population, belong to about thirty tribes, most of whom live in the south of Israel. Formerly nomadic, they are presently undergoing a transition to a sedentary society. (See chapter 3 for a more detailed discussion of Israeli Arabs.)

Other minorities comprise the remaining 2 percent of the total population. They include Druze, Circassian, and other small communities. The Druze are an independent religious community living in twenty-two villages in northern Israel. The community has existed since the early eleventh century when it broke away from Islam. There are also Druze communities in Syria and Lebanon. The Druze religion is monotheistic, but we know little else about it since its beliefs and practices are secret. We do know that the Druze believe in loyalty to the country in which they live. At the request of their own community leaders, service in the Israel Defense Forces (IDF) is mandatory for all Druze men. Circassians live in two villages in northern Israel. Although they are Muslims, they are not of Arab origin. Having come originally from the Caucasus Mountains of southern Russia, they migrated south and west from that area during the seventeenth and eighteenth centuries. Some settled in villages in the Galilee. Others moved on to become the ancestors of the Muslims in modern Bosnia. Circassians have maintained a distinct ethnic identity over the years.

The statistics cited above are helpful, but they only touch the surface. Making sense out of the Israeli mosaic—seeing that it fits together to form a picture—requires historical perspective.

The term "diaspora" comes from the Greek language. It means "dispersion" or "scattering" and is used to describe both an act (the dispersion of Jews to countries outside ancient Israel from the sixth century B.C., when Jews were exiled to Babylonia, until and including the present) and a group (the whole body of Jews or Jewish communities outside Palestine or modern Israel). Ever since the final dispersion of the Jews by the Romans in 70 A.D., the concept of the "ingathering of exiles" and the redemption of the Jewish people in their ancestral homeland have been a central part of Jewish tradition. Jews yearned and prayed for Zion and, throughout the ages, some pious Jews migrated to Israel. *Aliyah* (Hebrew for "ascent") meant a return to the Holy Land, the land of one's forefathers, and the termination of exile.

The Zionist Movement

After 1881, individual and group aliyah assumed a different character. To a large extent, the motivation of those who settled in Palestine from that time up to the mid-1920s was ideological rather than religious. Members of the Zionist movement, they came primarily from Russia and Poland in three major waves of immigration. Ethnically, the vast majority were virtually identical to the three million Jews who emigrated to the United States between 1881 and 1920, i.e., they were Ashkenazim—Jews of Eastern and Central European ancestry.

Why would a young man or woman choose to go to the

Middle East, a territory governed by the Ottoman Turks and later by the British, when most of his or her siblings or cousins were emigrating to the U.S.? The forces pushing the young immigrants out of Eastern Europe to the U.S. and the Middle East were identical: poverty, fear of conscription into the army of the czar, pogroms, and other expressions of anti-Semitism. The difference between the Jews who came to Palestine (later Israel) and those who emigrated to the United States lay in the forces that pulled them toward their respective destinations.

Modern Zionism, as distinguished from the traditional yearning for Zion, had a predominantly secular content. Its leaders were influenced by the socialist and nationalist doctrines espoused by various national groups in nineteenth-century Europe. Indeed, Zionism has been described as the national liberation movement of the Jewish people. It was one response to the oppression and persecution of Jews in Eastern Europe. And the Dreyfus Affair (involving the wrongful prosecution of a Jewish army officer) in 1890s France seemed to prove the possibility of assimilation in Western Europe an empty illusion. For the early Zionists, there was only one solution to the problem of Jewish survival: resettlement of Jews in their ancestral homeland and the eventual establishment of an independent Jewish state.

There were, of course, many ideological streams in the Zionist movement and much heated internecine feuding. Despite their differences, the Zionists shared a basic vision of the kind of community they wished to create. Their vision not only left an imprint on the Israeli character, to a large extent it determined what that character would be.[1]

---

[1] For a detailed discussion of the founding generation and a brilliant analysis of its role in shaping the Israeli character, see Amos Elon, *The Israelis: Founders and Sons*. Jerusalem: Adam, 1971, rev. 1981.

Patterns of Immigration

Although idealism and ideology have pulled many Jews to Palestine in every wave of immigration, it is also true that strong international forces have often limited their options.

After the mid-1920s, a number of countries which had previously accepted Jewish immigrants and refugees enacted restrictive immigration policies, the United States among them. Many Jews, pushed out of their homes in Europe, came to Palestine because they had no other choice.

Between 1924 and 1932, Polish anti-Semitism helped to produce the fourth wave of immigration. Sixty thousand Jews arrived in Palestine from Poland alone. The last major wave of immigration before World War II was that of German Jews escaping the anti-Semitism of Hitler's Germany. One hundred sixty-five thousand immigrants, who arrived between 1933 and 1939, were the first large-scale influx from Western Europe. Because of British restrictions on immigration after 1939, there was no major wave of immigration until the state was declared, though more than 140,000 immigrants did enter Palestine between 1939 and 1948. Many were brought in illegally, especially after 1945 when the British intensified their restrictions. They were primarily refugees from Nazi-occupied Europe and later, displaced people, survivors of Hitler's Final Solution. (The book *Exodus* by Leon Uris, and the movie made from it, have imprinted their dilemma in the minds of many Americans.)

By May 1948, when the British Mandate ended, the Jews in Palestine numbered 650,000. Ashkenazi Jews constituted more than 80 percent of the population. Although there were small enclaves of ultra-Orthodox Ashkenazi and Orthodox Sephardi Jews who maintained separate identities and institutions, the vast majority of Jews were non-Orthodox. Many of the Zionists who had arrived in the early waves of immigration were militantly secular. They built the political, military, and economic infrastructure of the Jewish state-in-the-

making and created the values and norms of what became
known as Labor Zionism. Labor Zionist pioneers dominated
Jewish organizations and institutions in Palestine: *kibbutzim*
(communal agricultural settlements), cooperatively owned
enterprises, the General Federation of Labor, the educational
and medical systems, and much more. They also created the
basis for a democratic political system and for an army.

Compared to the mass immigration of the post-World War
II era, the numbers in the prewar waves of immigration pale
in significance. By the end of 1951, only three years after it
had been created, the new state had absorbed over 685,000
new immigrants, more than doubling the number of Jews
living in Israel at the time of its independence. The new
immigrants included Holocaust survivors as well as over
300,000 "Oriental" (Eastern) Jews—those who came from
Muslim countries in North Africa and the Middle East. Life
for Jews in many of these countries had become untenable
after the Arab-Jewish wars of 1947-1948 and the creation of
the independent Jewish state in Israel, and more immigrants
were on the way. Between 1952 and 1964, over 300,000
additional Jews arrived from Islamic countries; in some cases,
entire Jewish communities were evacuated. Thus, approximately 600,000 Oriental Jews emigrated to Israel between
1948 and 1964.

The social consequences of the mass immigration of Jews
from Muslim countries were enormous: two Israels came into
being. The "First Israel" consisted of Ashkenazi Jews (old-
timers and newcomers) as well as a small number of Sephardi
families who had lived in Israel for generations. The term
"Sephardi Jews" is often used interchangeably with "Oriental
Jews." This is inaccurate. Used correctly, the term "Sephardi"
refers only to Jews descended from those who lived in Spain
and Portugal and were expelled in 1492 and 1498 respectively. They settled primarily in North Africa, although
smaller communities were established in Greece, Turkey, and
the Balkans. Some even filtered into northern Europe.

Sephardi Jews developed a culture and language—Ladino—parallel to, and as rich as, the Yiddish culture of the Ashkenazi Jews. Although Sephardi and Oriental Jews come from different backgrounds, they do share similar religious styles and other cultural characteristics.

The "Second Israel" was made up primarily of Oriental Jews. Many of the new immigrants were destitute. Their extended family structure was patriarchal, as was their social organization and political orientation. They were at home with traditional Judaism and resisted the attempts of the early settlers to modernize and secularize them. Israeli society, relatively homogeneous in 1948, mushroomed into an intricate mosaic of languages, colors, and customs. Ethnic and cultural differences were exacerbated by differences in socioeconomic status and access to political power.

Immigration to Israel did not, of course, cease with the mass immigration of the 1950s and early sixties. It has been a continuous process. During the 1970s, for example, more than 100,000 immigrants arrived from the former Soviet Union. Between 1984 and 1991, more than 30,000 Jews arrived from Ethiopia. Mass immigration from the former USSR resumed in 1989. Since that time, more than 543,000 immigrants have arrived from the former Soviet Union.

Perhaps a major difference between the American and the Israeli immigrant experiences lies in attitude. Trusting that time and social pressure would forge future generations into acceptable citizens, the United States tolerated cultural differences in the immigrant generation. Israeli leadership, on the other hand, intentionally adopted a policy of complete and immediate assimilation. Immigrants were to be divested of their Diaspora traits and transformed into Jews whose character would be the antithesis of their former selves. Why?

For many years, a major component of Zionist ideology was "negation of the Diaspora." When the early Zionists thought of the Diaspora, they associated it primarily with Jews in Christian Europe living on the periphery of non-Jewish society—people incapable of filling necessary roles in an independent Jewish state. Jews in the Diaspora were not "producers" (farmers, laborers) because these occupations were closed to them. Instead, they filled roles which feudal and church leaders determined were essential but demeaning to Christians: money lending, trade, and shopkeeping.

To make matters worse, Diaspora Jews were often dominated by the Orthodox Jewish religious leadership. In the analysis of the early Zionists, who had absorbed the antireligious ideas of nineteenth-century European socialism, Orthodoxy encouraged passivity and reinforced a victim mentality. This passivity prevented Jews from taking their fate actively into their own hands.

Zionist ideology, translated into norms and behavior patterns, *demanded* the creation of another kind of Jew. Thus, while building their own land, the Zionist pioneers were at the same time being built by it into a new kind of Jew, productive, self-sufficient, and powerful. ("Building and being built" was a powerful slogan encapsulating much of Zionist ideology.) They would not only be able to work the land and defend it, they would also be the factory workers, the police, and the street cleaners. In short, they would fill central roles in their own normal society, not peripheral roles in someone else's. Their Jewishness would be a component of their national, rather than their religious, identity. Most important, perhaps, was the issue of authority. For the first time in modern history, Jews would control their own national destiny. They would hold the reins of power in their own state.

For Jews who came after the early (primarily ideological) waves of immigration, social acceptance and economic survival dictated a special effort at adaptation. Many of the adults were neither motivated nor able to divest themselves of their cultural baggage and to thrust themselves into the melting pot to become the "new Jews" that the founding generation had envisioned.

For immigrant children and teenagers, the situation was different. The desire to be accepted by their sabra peers motivated most youngsters to blend in as quickly and completely as possible. In school, in youth movements, and later in the army, they made a concerted effort to take on the values, norms, and behavior patterns of their contemporaries.

Israel Today: Melting Pot, Salad Bowl, or Pressure Cooker?

For many years, immigrant absorption in Israel was synonymous with the melting pot. The extent to which the ingredients in the melting pot actually "melted" in the years during which Israel has been a state continues to arouse debate. What is indisputable is that the melting-pot model is now challenged (as it is in the U.S.) by the salad-bowl model of immigrant absorption.

In a salad, tomatoes, cucumbers, and onions exist side by side, but a tomato remains a tomato. It doesn't blend with the cucumbers into something different combining the two. The salad-bowl model suggests that the various groups manage to retain their ethnic identities. Today, many Israelis not only accept this model as a reflection of historical reality, they also believe that the salad-bowl model—the encouragement of social, ethnic, and cultural pluralism—should replace the melting pot as an ideal.

In certain respects, present-day Israel conforms to the definition of the salad bowl. The country consists of a varied mixture of communities identified by ethnicity, language, country of origin, social status, and class. Here are some examples:

A town in the north is populated mainly by North African immigrants as well as their native-born children and grandchildren. It is a "development town" established during the 1950s as a place to settle new immigrants. The children attend school in town. A few kilometers away is a kibbutz.

The population consists of the children, grandchildren, and great-grandchildren of the settlers who came from Eastern Europe in the early waves of immigration. The children attend school on the kibbutz. Their classmates are other kibbutz children, and their contact with the children in the development town is minimal. As far as the children in the town are concerned, the kibbutz could be on another planet. Next, Russian immigrants arrive in the development town, and it is impossible to go through the day without hearing Russian. The Russians establish their own community, and suddenly, the "them" and "us" of kibbutz and town changes to three different combinations of "them" and "us": within the town, between town and kibbutz, between old-timers and newcomers.

First-generation families of Russian, American, and Iraqi origin live in an upscale apartment building in a suburb. They exist in the salad, but they don't mix much with the other ingredients. Instead, they tend to maintain their strongest social connections with former immigrants like themselves—people who speak their native language and enjoy in common certain kinds of jokes, music, and sports.

Native-born Israelis from various ethnic backgrounds also live in the aforementioned suburb. They are in their forties and fifties, and they remember a time in the not-so-distant past when marriage between Ashkenazi and Oriental Jews created a stir. Indeed, such a liaison was viewed as intermarriage. Now, the children of the two groups speak the same language, go to the same schools, join youth movements together, listen to the same rock and roll, attend the same parties and universities, and serve together in the army. They think of themselves as Israelis, not Moroccans or Poles; intermarriage, in this context, has become a meaningless concept. However, just when it seems that the salad bowl is transforming itself into a melting pot, fresh ingredients are added. New groups of immigrants arrive.

The United States and Israel share several salad-bowl characteristics. Yet the United States is so big that, in many locations, it may still be possible to go through an entire day without meeting someone who speaks another language or comes from a different ethnic background. Israel, on the other hand, is the size of New Jersey. Daily "bumping up" against someone from another culture is a given.

The bumping up often has a tolerant, live-and-let-live character, an acceptance of ethnic and cultural differences. Differences between groups are seen as the natural order of things. On the other hand, the flavors in the Israeli salad bowl sometimes clash. Ethnic and cultural differences produce friction. Live-and-let-live becomes "us" and "them." When this happens, the great Israeli salad bowl makes a startling metaphorical leap and is transformed into a *pressure cooker!*

Sometimes the "us" and "them" in the pressure cooker refers to ethnic groups, particularly Ashkenazi and Oriental Jews. Many Oriental Jews look back on the period of the 1950s and 1960s with bitterness. They view those years as a time when they were systematically humiliated and discriminated against by the Ashkenazi establishment, particularly by the dominant labor movement. They were housed in tents or transit camps, and many were settled in new development towns and agricultural communities in the Galilee and Negev—areas far from population centers and, except for the kibbutzim, from Ashkenazi old-timers. The labor-movement establishment was also blamed for what some viewed as a deliberate policy of maintaining social, educational, and economic gaps and keeping Oriental Jews from positions of power.

Both the political and economic pictures began to change in the 1970s. Since that time, Oriental Jews have been increasingly represented in the centers of power—the Knesset (Israel's national legislature), local government, and political parties—as well as the professions, academia, labor unions, and the army officer corps. A turning point came in the 1977 national elections when the dominant Labor party was defeated for the first time in Israeli political history.

Yet a number of issues remain unresolved. To what extent have Oriental Jews really been absorbed into the mainstream? Is the "mainstream" Ashkenazi? If so, what does it mean to be "absorbed"? Conversely, to what extent has the Ashkenazi mainstream been influenced by the culture of Oriental Jews? To what extent have the frustration, alienation, and poverty of their early years in the country been reduced? To what extent have Oriental Jews truly moved into the middle class and become integrated into the top ranks of government, military, and cultural life? In short, does the Second Israel still exist? (Interestingly, the term itself seems to have disappeared from the Israeli lexicon.) Since these issues continue to elicit debate in Israeli society, answers will depend on whom you ask and how you phrase your question.

What is true is that Ashkenazi and Oriental politicians are usually careful not to let the ethnic genie out of the bottle. Sometimes it escapes, however. The arrival in recent years of over half a million Jews from the former Soviet Union has reignited smoldering ethnic bitterness, exacerbated by cultural and religious differences. Here's an example:

Kiryat Shmonah is a development town in the north of Israel. Most of the town's residents are Oriental Jews—sons, daughters, and grandchildren of Orthodox Jews who emigrated from North Africa. They tend to be traditional rather than Orthodox, respectful of Jewish law but not strictly observant in all ritual detail. They may attend the synagogue on Sabbath morning and a football game in the afternoon.

During the past few years, a number of Russian immigrants have settled in Kiryat Shmonah. Products of a Communist state, they tend to be secular in the extreme. One of the new immigrants recently opened a pork shop in town, something legal but previously unheard of. Old-time residents are having great difficulty coming to terms with such a blatant violation of local norms. They have picketed the shop, and the city council has passed an ordinance banning the selling of pork within city limits. The shop's owner, proud of her economic success in her new country, cannot understand the old-timers' revulsion.

The pressure-cooker atmosphere also comes from political disagreements between religious and secular Jews. There are times when the two groups face each other as adversaries in the ongoing debate about the Jewishness of the Jewish state.

Here's an example:

Since the early years of the state, places of entertainment have been closed on the Sabbath, which begins on Friday night. (See chapter 2 for a detailed discussion of the "blue laws.") In recent years, however, several cities and towns have acceded to secular demands and opened movie theaters and discos on Friday night. The ultra-Orthodox and modern Orthodox communities have objected. Although their objections have usually taken the form of peaceful demonstrations, there have been instances in which ultra-Orthodox demonstrations have turned into riots against the police and, by extension, the state itself. Secular Jews then lump all religious Jews together, saying: "The Orthodox are trying to create a fundamentalist state." Modern Orthodox and ultra-Orthodox Jews retort: "The nonreligious are destroying centuries of Jewish tradition. By the time they're finished, there will be nothing Jewish about the Jewish state!"

If Israel looks like a salad bowl and feels like a pressure cooker, whatever happened to the melting pot? We believe that it remains a valid metaphor for explaining the way Israeli society functions. The melting-pot policy of the early Zionist leaders may not have produced the results they envisaged, but it probably succeeded more than their critics admit. There are factors in Israel which lend cohesion and promote a common culture. Some of these, the public schools, for example, are common to every society. Three factors, however, are unique to Israel. They are: the army, the Jewishness of the state, and "the situation."

The Army

Several times a year, one can witness the following scene at the local army induction center:

Hundreds of young men are waiting to hear their names called. They will then board buses for transport to "Bakum"— the central base for induction and classification. One hears the colloquial Hebrew of young sabras as well as the babel of languages of the many immigrant parents. An entire *chevreh*, or gang of buddies, has come to see their friend off (knowing that their turn is only a few months away). Parents as well as brothers and sisters are busy posing for pictures, adjusting their Polaroid or video cameras. The inductees are embracing girlfriends; mothers (and fathers too) may have tears in their eyes. There are young religious men with *kipot* (skullcaps) as well as inductees who, until this day, had virtually no contact with anyone who could be defined as Orthodox. A well-to-do attorney from a prestigious suburb discovers that the sons of two of his clients are being inducted the same day; another parent, a garage mechanic, discovers that the son of his doctor is boarding the bus along with his own son; a middle-class matron meets her cleaning lady whose son is also waiting for the roll call.

This is the quintessential Israeli scene because the army is the nearly universal Israeli experience. "To be an Israeli adult is to be a soldier."[2] Service in the IDF is compulsory. Indeed, Israel has longer universal compulsory military service than any other Western country. Young men and women enter the army at age eighteen. Women serve in the army for twenty-two months. (Israel is the only country in the world in which women do compulsory army service.) Men serve for three years. Officers and members of special units serve for four years or longer. At least 80 percent of the eighteen-year-old

---

[2] Reuven Gal, A *Portrait of the Israeli Soldier*. New York: Greenwood Press, 1986, 33.

male manpower pool is inducted each year.[3]

After they finish regular army service, male soldiers are placed in reserve units in which they serve some twenty-five to thirty years. Women are released from reserve duty at the age of twenty-four. Most reservists are called to active duty for a total of at least thirty-five days annually, frequently more for officers. It is not unusual for a father to be in reserve duty at the same time that his son is in compulsory service.

The influence of the army on Israeli life is far-reaching. It may be the first occasion that secular and religious Israelis find themselves in the same group; and, of course, it may be the first time youngsters from upscale suburbs share living quarters with individuals from the inner city, and kibbutzniks are thrown together with sophisticated Tel Avivians. The army is also considered the country's most successful matchmaker, the place where scores of young men and women meet their future mates.

In addition, and perhaps more significantly, the army also reflects and reinforces Israeli norms. It is as much a part of the socialization process for native-born Israelis as it is for new immigrants and their families. When they leave the army, soldiers often transfer army norms, values, and behavior patterns to civilian life. The annual reserve duty reinforces the impact of the early socialization process.

Most immigrants who arrived in Israel when they were adolescents report that they became "real Israelis" during/ because of their army experience. They left their old ways behind because they wanted to adapt and become accepted by Israelis, or because *not* abandoning those ways meant that they would never advance. At the very least, keeping the old ways guaranteed a miserable army experience.

---

[3] Though both men and women serve in the IDF, they are inducted and trained separately. The scene we've described is repeated when young women recruits leave for the army. See chapter 3 for a detailed description of women in the army.

In the army, sabras and immigrants alike go through a rite of passage into Israeli adulthood. Soldiers who come from lower socioeconomic backgrounds find that successful army service, usually translated as being an NCO or junior officer in a combat unit, enhances their upward social mobility. The army is thus a ticket *up* for sabras and a ticket *in* for immigrants.

This is less true for women. Women in the army don't have the same opportunities for bonding that men do, and they aren't tested in training or combat in the same way as men. (See chapter 3.)

Virtually all the Israeli cultural characteristics discussed in the following chapters find expression in the IDF. Key examples include:

Egalitarianism. This value expresses itself in a lack of distance between leaders and led. There are no officer academies or academic prerequisites for officers' courses. Officers come up through the ranks; every soldier has an opportunity to become an officer. Soldiers share the same duties until those who have proven themselves are selected for officers' training courses. In camp or in the field, officers and soldiers almost always share the same facilities, eat the same food, and endure the same conditions.

Group cohesion. Basic training focuses on the group or squad of ten to twelve members. In many instances, Israelis go through their entire military service with the same people who formed their group in basic training or the specialization course immediately following. The cohesiveness and camaraderie in military units give them a distinct advantage under fire. However, in this respect as in many others, the army reflects the values that soldiers picked up in school and youth activities. From an early age, children are encouraged to develop strong friendships and a sense of belonging to a cohesive group.

Lack of ceremony. One could argue that the Israeli military has a distinct aversion to formality, pomp, and circumstance.

Creative thinking, initiative, and improvisation in the face of new and unexpected situations.[4]

Jewishness

Jerusalem 1988. Masses of people are standing in line. Some have arrived in the early hours of the morning in order to be sure that there will be room for them inside the auditorium. The crowd is secular and religious, Ashkenazi and Sephardi, "greenhorn" immigrants and third-generation sabras, high-school students and old-timers in their seventies. They are waiting to be admitted to the trial of John Demjanjuk, accused of being "Ivan the Terrible," the one-time Nazi death-camp guard. The proceedings are broadcast live on radio. One can hear it on buses, in grocery stores, and in offices throughout the country. Bus drivers, garage mechanics, and professors are riveted to the news even if no one in their respective families perished in the Holocaust. The trial is the main topic of conversation between taxi drivers and passengers, clerks and customers, managers and workers. (In 1993, after several years of the trial and appeals process, Demjanjuk was released. The Israeli Supreme Court ruled that the prosecution had not proved that he was in fact guilty of the crimes with which he was charged.)

Ironically, the same Jewishness which turns Israel into a potentially explosive pressure cooker also acts as a cohesive force. Regardless of their origins, most Israelis share a common historical memory *as Jews*. They also share the experience of living in the only Jewish country in the world.

What does it mean to live in a Jewish state?

---

[4] For an in-depth discussion of the role of the army in Israeli culture, we suggest Gal, *Portrait*. Group cohesiveness and the crystallization metaphors are addressed by Tamar Katriel in *Communal Webs: Communication and Culture in Contemporary Israel*. Albany: State University of New York Press, 1991.

First, there are the things that every newcomer notices:

The calendar. The Sabbath, the official day of rest, is on Saturday (actually Friday sundown until Saturday sundown), not Sunday, as it is in the Christian world, nor Friday, as it is observed in the Muslim world. School holidays and semester breaks are scheduled according to the Hebrew calendar, which dates from Genesis and is based on the lunar year. It includes biblical festivals as well as those that developed through the millennia and results, for instance, in the Jewish New Year, Rosh Hashanah, falling on a day in September or October of the Roman calendar. Business, however, is conducted according to the Roman calendar with which Americans are familiar. If you are corresponding with an Orthodox Jew or a government office, you may find two dates on a letter—one according to the Hebrew calendar, the other according to the Roman calendar. Israelis celebrate every Jewish holiday, even some that American Jews have never heard of! American newcomers who arrive in the country in the fall are often amazed to come upon the pre-Jewish New Year last-minute shopping hysteria they usually associate with Christmas. In Israel, knowledge of non-Jewish holidays is minimal.

National symbols. The Union Jack of Great Britain is composed of the crosses of several Christian saints. Israel's national flag is patterned on the *tallit*, the Jewish prayer shawl; and its state seal, comparable to America's bald eagle, is the seven-branched *menorah* (candelabra) originally used in the ancient temple in Jerusalem. Coins, currency, stamps, and other tangible expressions of nationhood depict personalities or scenes from Jewish history.

Language. The major national language is Hebrew. Both Arabic and Hebrew are designated official languages, but Hebrew is the language known and used by almost all Israelis. It is an established norm that Israeli Arabs are expected to speak Hebrew; Israeli Jews are not expected to speak Arabic. What is special about Hebrew? It is the language of the

Jewish Bible, known in most of the Western world as the Old Testament. Hebrew virtually died as a spoken language during most of the 1,800 years of the Jewish Diaspora. It was revived in the late nineteenth-early twentieth century, and Israeli Jews take great pride in the daily use of the same language used by King David in writing his psalms and by Isaiah in composing his sermons.

Education. Sojourners whose children are enrolled in Israeli schools find that ancient and modern Jewish history are an integral part of the curriculum. Emphasis is placed on the effect developments in world history had on Jewish communities. An American immigrant, a former history teacher, was delighted when her son began studying ancient history. Finally, she would be able to help him with his homework. She was surprised to discover, however, that the Roman emperors studied in depth by Israeli students are those who had the biggest impact on the ancient Hebrew kingdom of Judea. Those same emperors may receive little or no mention in the ancient history textbooks that American students use. In Israeli schools, for example, Vespasian is more important than Julius Caesar.

Attitude. The mere fact of growing up Jewish in the *only* Jewish country in the world produces a unique set of attitudes. Virtually all visitors have something to say about the extraordinary self-confidence that Israelis display. We must have heard the following comments at least five hundred times: "These guys walk around like they own the place!" (they do); "Didn't it ever occur to them that there's something they can't do?" (not noticeably); "Aren't they afraid of anything?" (of course they are). Growing up as part of a majority—in contrast to the generations and generations of Jews who grew up as part of an often persecuted minority—has had an effect on the demeanor of Israelis as well as on their self-image.

In the Diaspora, even in the U.S., Jews behave the way minorities often do. They develop a sensitivity to the subtlest anti-Semitic or racist slight and a special armor which allows them to fend it off. It is dangerous to remove the armor; one must remain vigilant, on guard. Despite the armor, however, Jews often feel personally vulnerable and hyperconscious of the impression they make on non-Jews. They can't help asking themselves "What will non-Jews think?" every time another Jew does or says something that non-Jews might find distasteful, especially if it appears in the press.

In Israel, both vulnerability and vigilance have undergone a subtle but clear change. The "what will they think?" issue has diminished; after all, Jews are not the minority here. The tools and trappings of state power provide a measure of physical and psychological security. Israelis know that collectively they remain vulnerable, but they are not helpless. They can defend themselves because they have a mechanism, the state, with which to fight back. Yet the impulse to be vigilant remains.

As Jews, Israelis still can't help being a little suspicious of the outsider, of "them." In the background is the in-group cohesiveness reinforced over centuries by the feeling of separateness and the accumulated experiences of anti-Semitism. When they look at the history of the Jewish Diaspora, Israelis find few reasons to trust the non-Jewish world. A predictable pattern almost always repeated itself. Periods of peaceful coexistence, even a flowering of Jewish culture and assimilation into the non-Jewish world, were almost always followed by periods of anti-Jewish discriminatory laws and/or violence. This pattern has been less true in the U.S. than in other parts of the world, and Jews who have grown up in the U.S. often look at Jewish history differently from those who are products of other Diaspora experiences.

The insider/outsider or "us versus them" phenomenon is not unique to Israel. It appears in all human societies. For centuries, it has been the norm rather than the exception in the Middle East, exacerbated by the complex relationship between cultures and nations. Individuals may be citizens of

Jordan, Syria, Lebanon, or Iraq, for example, but their ethnic, tribal, and religious identities have usually been more important than their national identities. Hafez Al Assad, ruler of Syria, comes from a minority religious sect—the Alawites. Yet Alawites hold virtually all significant positions of power in Syria. Whom else could Assad trust except his own kinsmen? In the Middle East, people tend to accept this situation as the natural order of things.

Fifty years of armed warfare also play a role in placing "them" in a negative light. When Israelis meet a stranger, they (jokingly or seriously) ask the question: "Is he or she 'one of ours'?" In other words, a subtle filtering process is at work. It determines who can get close and who stays out in the cold. (In chapter 5, we will apply this phenomenon to the concentric-circles model of intimacy-distance.)

"The Situation" (Ha Matzav)

"The situation" is reflected on the front pages of every daily newspaper. It refers to a state of perpetual tension brought on by a daily blend of threats and surprises. The state of tension in which Israelis live comes from a never-ending sense of uncertainty regarding the security of the country. Details of "the situation"—threats from the Arab world, terrorist incidents, trouble on the border, economic dislocations caused by the security situation—may change from day to day, as do the newspaper headlines, but the constant barrage has an immediate and continuing effect on everyone.

In September 1993, Israel and the PLO signed a declaration of principles. In it, they formally recognized each other and agreed to enter a negotiation process involving the modalities of a Palestinian autonomy, the initial stages of which would include the Jericho district and parts of the Gaza Strip. However, the agreement has not at all altered the Israeli sense of uncertainty about the security of the country and, increasingly, about their personal security. It is unlikely to do so in the immediate future.

Israel and the PLO have embarked on a lengthy process of transforming an agreement on paper into a reality on the ground. Sizable numbers of both Israelis and Palestinians are convinced that the agreement jeopardizes their existence and some are making every effort to ensure that it fails. Even those who support the agreement are experiencing the predictable ups and downs inherent in any major political transformation. Hopes are raised, dashed, raised again, dashed again. It's hard to predict with any certainty what the future holds for Israelis and Palestinians. The Old Testament seers may have possessed the gift of prophecy. For present-day Israelis, it's a dangerous calling.

Militarily, Israelis live on the edge. The feeling that one is physically threatened is never far from the surface. At any given time, virtually every family in the country has someone serving in the army. As the hourly newscast approaches, tension—in offices, on buses, and elsewhere—becomes palpable. There is a shared sense of concern that yet another soldier has been injured or killed, very possibly somebody from *my* neighborhood, *my* community, *my* family.

Because everyone is affected by "the situation," it produces a common mindset. Israelis are accustomed to living with limited resources, under conditions in which things are always in a state of flux. People are used to surprises. They feel that something will always happen to threaten them, to dry up the resources, or to upset the little sense of stability that exists at any given moment. The ability to improvise becomes a survival skill, and short-term planning becomes a way of life. Because they live on the edge and are confident that they can cope with any situation that may arise, Israelis develop a positive attitude toward risk taking. Indeed, the common belief that "the situation" affects everyone and the shared attitude of "we can deal with it" lend remarkable cohesiveness to Israeli society.

By now, the picture in the Israeli jigsaw puzzle should be

taking shape. Because of its history—the imprint made by the founding generation and continuous waves of immigration that followed—the society is diverse. Religious and ethnic differences threaten at times to tear it apart, yet there are significant elements which provide cohesion and produce a national culture.

First Impressions

The first few hours, the first few days, in any new culture are often critical for newcomers. In this chapter, we examine these first impressions. Our comments are based on reports of what first-time sojourners to Israel saw and heard during their initial encounter with Israeli society. We'll focus particularly on the contrast between what the newcomers expected to see and what they actually experienced—and the resulting confusion and disorientation they felt. Many things in Israel are ambiguous, and mixed messages are the rule rather than the exception. Let's start out with a description of the first impressions of a visitor just arrived from the United States.

The Ben Yehuda Pedestrian Mall

I arrived with my partner early in the morning on a flight from New York. We went directly to our hotel in Jerusalem to sleep off our jet lag, but before we could get to bed, our host called and invited us to relax with him for a while at an outdoor cafe. Surprised and delighted, we accepted and soon found ourselves on the Ben Yehuda pedestrian mall in downtown Jerusalem.

I cannot remember a place in which I received so many

different impressions in so short a time. I was bombarded by contradictory stimuli. After a while, feeling somewhat over-whelmed, I gave up trying to interpret these impressions. I sat back and let my senses take in what they could—a kaleido-scope of sights, sounds, smells, tastes, and tactile sensations. Then I took notes, writing down those things which stood out and intrigued me most. I kept the notes so that I could ask questions later.

- Soldiers, uniforms, rifles, submachine guns. Patrolling, in downtown Jerusalem?! And other soldiers sitting in the cafe or kidding around. Women soldiers, too. So many soldiers. Scary. Civilians with pistols too—feels like the Wild West.

- Movement, action, tension, wariness, crowding. Lots of physical contact: walking, bumping into people. Hard to walk ten steps in a straight line without a collision, or a violent twist to avoid one. Even those sitting at the tables at the cafe are in constant motion, tapping the rhythm of the music from radios.

- Noise: radios or cassettes from the shops, street musi-cians, loud conversations, vehicles on nearby roads, kids shouting, construction.

- Lots of kids: parents out with children—sometimes whole families together; baby strollers; older children—look like fifth or sixth graders, in groups of three to six out on their own—venturing downtown. The attitude of adults toward children is accepting, amused toler-ance; one child falls and scrapes his knee, another loses her mother—they are not ignored; instead, are hugged and helped by bystanders.

- Flirting; no, deeper than that, an open acceptance of sexuality; not just dress and jewelry, but the way people hold and move their bodies, proud, unashamed. Re-minds me more of a Mediterranean promenade in Greece, Italy, or southern France than the Middle East of Cairo or Damascus. My host says that this is nothing. Wait till we get to Tel Aviv. That's *really* Mediterranean.

- Litter: kids throwing candy wrappers on the ground. No, too much paper and other stuff; it can't all be from children; it's really dirty here! The tables and chairs at the cafe are clean but scratched plastic, and the umbrellas which shade us from the sun have definitely seen better days and many previous seasons.

- Skin colors: from Scandinavian white-and-blond to deep African black, tans, reds, desert-burned leather browns—all mixed up in the semirandom movement of the promenade.

- Languages: Hebrew mostly, but English too in various accents; French, Spanish, Russian; others that I can't identify.

- Food: folks eating or drinking as they walk—ice cream, candy bars, nuts, seeds, fruits, colas—and every two feet, it seems, another kiosk invites you to indulge. Lots of overhanging bellies too; the basketball bellies on the men here are different from the spare tires of overweight Americans.

- Costumes: tourist groups with cameras and identical, brightly colored hats, virtually everyone carrying some kind of bag—purse, knapsack, briefcase, even plastic bags. Everything from short shorts and high heels to neat and clean undershirts to blue jeans, sandals, and bow ties; sloppiness and elegance. Even the elegance is informal; very few ties, suits, tailored dresses, or anything else confining.

- Those must be the ultra-Orthodox I have read so much about: men dressed in black, almost all with a beard. Except for the earlocks hanging down, they remind me of the Amish in Pennsylvania. There are also some couples. The ultra-Orthodox women have their heads covered. They wear stockings and dark, long dresses with long sleeves. Two such couples are surrounded by children, obviously families, their behavior different from the other family groups on the mall: they stay together, kids not running out and back like yo-yos, as they do in other families; the Orthodox are clearly not lingering to enjoy themselves.

- Lots of men with different kinds of skullcaps—silk, knitted with designs, some all black. Any significance to the differences?

- An older woman enters the scene with a plastic bag filled with vegetables which she offers for sale as she moves from one group to another. She is wearing a long embroidered dress and I assume she is an Arab.

All of a sudden, I realize several things simultaneously. First, all the people around me are Jewish. While I know intellectually that Israel is a Jewish country with a majority of Jews in its population, I only now begin to absorb the meaning of being in the only country in the world in which Jews create the prevailing culture, and non-Jews constitute the minority. Second, while I know that practically all the people around me are Jewish, most are so different from the Jews I'm familiar with at home that I didn't make the connection until just now. Third, even though I have read so much about Jews and Arabs living together in Israel, I realize that I have not seen any Arabs. Not that I would be sure what they look like unless they wore clearly identifiable costumes, as did this woman. And what is the appropriate terminology? Is she "Palestinian" or "Arab"? And whom do I ask?

There are so many things here that are potentially sensitive. Do I dare open my mouth to make a comment or ask a question, or will I put my foot in it?

I decide that my host, who invited us to the mall in the first place, is no dummy. He must expect this experiential overload of first impressions to overflow into questions. I take a deep breath and begin to ask....

Can all these people really be Jews? If you are looking for that perfect bagel, or the best deli in the world, or some other replication of an American Yiddish-speaking "old Jewish neighborhood," you won't find it in Israel.

Nothing of your experience as a Jew in America, or in your interactions with Jews, or what you may have heard about Jews has prepared you for dealing with the reality you will meet in Israel. Regardless of how much you have read about Israel and the "ingathering of the exiles" from more than eighty countries, it is normal to arrive expecting Jews in Israel to resemble the Jews you are familiar with in the United States. Most don't. Nor are they *doing* the things you expect them to be doing.

Israelis are of many national and ethnic origins. After generations of ethnic mixing, Jews whose families have been hundreds of years in Yemen, Iraq, Ethiopia, India, North Africa, or even Scandinavia have returned to Israel with the physical features of the natives of those societies.

In Israel, most of the people at the airport, most of the people filling the streets of Tel Aviv and Jerusalem—the first destinations for most sojourners—are Jews. There are Jewish soldiers, bus drivers, policemen and policewomen, grocery clerks, street vendors, even pickpockets and prostitutes. The early Zionist goal of creating "a normal people in a normal society" is on its way to realization.

What happens to American Jews in Israel? Is their response to Israeli culture different from that of non-Jewish Americans? American Jews have religious/spiritual connections as well as cultural-historical ties to their ancient homeland. In their interactions with modern Israelis, however, American Jews experience communication and adjustment problems, just as other Americans do.

Religious/spiritual and cultural-historical connections, however deeply felt, provide little preparation for encountering modern-day Israelis and Israeli culture. Jews who come to Israel for extended visits, e.g., professional assignments and study-abroad programs, expect to feel at home and comfortable with Israelis who will be welcoming and helpful. "They are, after all, my brothers and sisters, fellow Jews." Instead, they discover that Israelis are not like American Jews at all, and Israel really is a different country whose citizens behave in foreign ways. Indeed, the most frequently heard lament among American Jews in Israel is, "In the U.S., I felt Jewish. In Israel, I feel like an American." And, irony of ironies, Israelis use the term "Anglo-Saxons" to refer to visitors and immigrants from all English-speaking countries whether or not they are Jewish.

The sensation of not being treated as a member of the family can be surprising and painful. It is often accompanied by the realization, "I am as foreign to them as they are to me." That's true. American Jews' speech and behavior patterns are those of other Americans, and Israelis see them primarily as Americans. (It helps if they speak Hebrew even though the language issue can sometimes boomerang. American accents tend to stand out and may cause language-conscious Israelis to wince. However, Israelis appreciate the effort to learn their language and are likely to be more open to Hebrew speakers.)

The result: The cultural adjustment process experienced by all long-term visitors, Jews and non-Jews alike, takes on an added poignancy. Once the initial euphoria dissipates and culture shock sets in, many American Jews report feelings of confusion. "It's my homeland, but I don't feel at home yet." Or: "I feel at home in Israel, but I don't feel comfortable with Israelis." In time, of course, most of these reactions diminish in intensity or disappear. Indeed, many Jewish long-term sojourners and immigrants have notable success assimilating into Israeli society. Sometimes, however, the gap between American-Jewish expectations and Israeli reality fails to disappear completely.

We have frequently been asked whether there is any particular advantage or disadvantage in sending an American Jew on assignment to Israel. Our response, borne out by experience, is that it has no greater or lesser advantage than sending an Irish American on assignment to Ireland or an Italian American to Italy. Israelis are interested primarily in the professional competence of the individual; ethnic or religious identity is not a critical issue.

Shouldn't everybody here be religious? Why would Jews want to live in Israel or help build a Jewish country if they weren't religious in the first place? One hears this from many American newcomers, Jews and non-Jews alike. Even among the most sophisticated, the expectation exists that most Israelis will be ritually observant and that their Jewishness will be connected to religious practice. ("Observant" Jews are those who regularly perform religious rituals.)

The early Zionists rejected the definition of Jewishness which confined itself to membership in a religious group only, a definition which had been accepted in the European Diaspora for some one hundred years. They chose to redress the situation by effecting a change in the collective mentality of the Jewish people. Jewish identity would become synonymous with national identity, and Jews—after two millennia in the Diaspora—would take their place in their own homeland as "a normal nation among the nations of the world."

As noted in chapter 1, the leaders of the Zionist movement were revolutionaries, liberal or socialist in their political theory, and secular in outlook. Indeed, many individuals in the founding generation weren't only secular, they were antireligious. Since the founders controlled all the dominant institutions of the pre-state Jewish community in Palestine as well as those of the new state after 1948, they succeeded not only in creating the Jewish state, but also in carrying out the social and cultural revival of Jewish national life. The result was several generations of "new Jews," who turned into Israelis, for whom national identity and patriotism were often more important than Jewish ritual life.

No revolution is as pure as its leaders would like it to be. The intentions of the founding generation notwithstanding, the Jewish community in Palestine (later Israel) was overwhelmed by successive waves of immigration which brought Jews of different backgrounds and religious traditions into the country. The religious and cultural patterns of these immigrants created a new reality, one that Israeli society has been dealing with ever since.

In addition, a modern religious Zionist movement, combining political Zionism with a reinterpreted orthodoxy, developed in the 1930s. The religious Zionists created institutions parallel to those of the secular pioneers, e.g., schools and youth movements. Many of the new immigrants were able to identify more easily with religious Zionism than with the secular Zionism of the earlier settlers.

Recent studies reveal that the Jewish population of Israel today can be distributed along a spectrum from the ultra-Orthodox at one end to the actively antireligious at the other end. The great middle majority are respectful, even observant of, some Jewish traditions and rituals, though interpretations of observance vary widely. And that same middle majority is tolerant of religious diversity.

Ethnic groups tend to cluster at different points on the religious-secular spectrum: Jews of North African background, for example, tend to be on the religious-traditional side; Jews from the former Soviet Union tend to be on the secular side.

If the country is as diverse as you describe, why do I sometimes get the feeling that there is a strong Jewish religious presence? The feeling you'll have about the general atmosphere in Israel will depend on what you see, whom you see, and where you are. During your sojourn in Israel, you are likely to see the Orthodox and ultra-Orthodox frequently on television or to read about them in the press. The Orthodox and ultra-Orthodox hold political power based on their swing-vote leverage in

Israel's parliamentary system, where they can make and break government coalitions. Their concerns become objects of news analysis and reporting so that the general public can understand the religious parties' policies and demands. The phenomenon of religious political parties is not unique to Israel. Christian and Catholic democratic parties exist in numerous European and Latin American countries.

You'll also notice additional signs of the religious presence in everyday Israeli life:

In many hotels and restaurants, a certificate is prominently displayed in the front window or foyer. This is a notification to the public that the food served is kosher, that is, prepared and served according to the requirements of Jewish dietary law. In these places, you will not be able to order a meal with both milk and meat products, nor will you be able to order shellfish, pork, or other foods designated as unclean.

On the Sabbath—Friday sundown until Saturday sundown, as noted earlier—El Al Airlines, Israel Railroads, the public bus cooperatives, and other government-owned or partially owned transportation systems do not operate. Most businesses are closed as well. In many areas of the country, places of entertainment are also shut down.

On the right doorpost of many rooms and buildings you'll see a small tube or rectangular box known as a *mezuzah*. This is a hollow artifact containing a piece of parchment on which are written Hebrew phrases from scripture. A mezuzah can be found at the entrance to homes, supermarkets, schools and other public buildings, factories and offices. Orthodox and many traditional Jews reach out and touch the mezuzah every time they go through a doorway, and often then kiss their fingers. This behavior holds different meanings for different Jews, as similar ritual behaviors do for adherents of other religious traditions. It may be a significant religious act, reaffirming one's commitment to God and to keeping the commandments. It may be a ritual gesture, more or less empty of immediate meaning, but a habit difficult to break. Or it may have become a superstitious gesture propitiating "the un-known and mysterious" forces which prevent bad luck from crossing the threshold.

Your commercial, bureaucratic, professional, and social interactions will be with both secular and modern Orthodox Israelis. Jews identified as modern Orthodox are integrated into virtually all walks of Israeli life—political parties, the army, and the professions. The men wear skullcaps whose fabric and design identify the wearer as a member of one religious/political movement or another. Otherwise, their appearance is identical to that of secular Israelis. Married women also wear head coverings; indeed, you may be sur-prised to see women wearing hats indoors.

Tradition requires Jews to pray in communal services three times per day. A quorum or *minyan* of ten men is necessary. It's possible that some of the Orthodox Jews attending a meeting in which you are participating may quietly excuse themselves in order to join the prayer service. Or someone will request that one of the secular participants excuse him-self from the meeting so that he can be the tenth man at the minyan, i.e., help to form the required quorum. Some organi-zations have designated a specific room as a synagogue. Oth-ers allow employees to use a conference room on a regular basis. You are more likely to come across this phenomenon in Jerusalem than in Tel Aviv. (See page 41.)

Your first impressions will prove accurate. There is, in-deed, a strong, visible, religious presence in all areas of Israeli public life. How did such a situation come about in a state created essentially by secular, socialist Zionists? The answer lies in the demands of coalition politics and the necessities of symbolic compromise.

In 1947, on the eve of independence, David Ben Gurion, then leader of the resoundingly secular Zionist labor move-ment and head of the government-in-waiting, signed an agree-ment with the ultra-Orthodox parties. In order to gain their support for the United Nations partition plan, and to avoid

alienating Jewish communities around the world, Ben Gurion
made several concessions to the Orthodox community. In the
new state, the Sabbath would be the official day of rest, the
government would support religious education, and matters
of personal status, e.g., marriage and divorce, would be under
the jurisdiction of the religious courts. This agreement became the basis of a series of blue laws, or what later became
known as the "status quo." Over the years, coalition politics
has resulted in the passage of several laws of importance to
the religious parties. Almost all of these are still on the
books. They relate to many of the above areas and include
legislation providing public financing for Orthodox religious
institutions as well as laws prohibiting public transportation
on the Sabbath, allowing local authorities to ban entertainment on the Sabbath, and prohibiting the importation of
nonkosher meat. Legislation exempting ultra-Orthodox young
men from conscription into the IDF so that they can devote
themselves to religious study is also part of the status quo.

The assumption behind the status quo was that the situation as it existed in the areas discussed in the agreement
would be maintained. However, the status quo has been altered numerous times in a variety of ways. The ultra-Orthodox, who, since 1977, have taken on an increasingly powerful
role in coalition governments, have pressed for stricter religious laws, e.g., banning "provocative" advertising and limit-
ing the conditions under which abortions can be performed.

When it comes to the question of religious issues in the
political arena, Israelis respond in "either/or" and "for/against"
dichotomies. Those on the "against" side distinguish between
their respect for centuries-old tradition, ritual, and values
and the antipathy they feel toward the Orthodox parties and
the rabbinical bureaucracy. They align themselves according
to whether they support or resist political attempts by Orthodox and ultra-Orthodox parties to impose religious law on
the entire population and to increase government allocations
for Orthodox institutions. The "against" in this dichotomy

includes all those who oppose state imposition of religious norms. Many people in this group are themselves observant Jews. When some Israeli Jews express their frustrations by declaring "I can't stand the religious," they are probably referring to this political dichotomy and the public debate which is dominated by spokespeople for the two extremes.

To a certain extent, every Jewish city and town in Israel struggles with the issues described above. Each one must continually balance the competing forces of religious sensitivity, good neighborliness, coalition politics in the local city council, and freedom of choice when dealing with the needs of different Jewish populations.

There are some places in Israel where the prevailing lifestyle is secular, others where the religious lifestyle dominates. As a visitor, you'll probably find that Tel Aviv and Jerusalem represent contrasting models.

Jerusalem. Thirty percent of the Jewish population is ultra-Orthodox, and that percentage is growing. There is also a sizable modern Orthodox population. You'll find that the ambience varies from place to place within the city (on the Ben Yehuda mall, you can take in the entire religious-secular spectrum), but the city tends to be religious. How can it not be? Jerusalem is a holy city for Jews, Christians, and Muslims. One can spend months just visiting all the religious sites.

You'll see many men in skullcaps. The ultra-Orthodox, known as *haredim* (God-fearing), are also clearly identifiable. The men in some of the sects have a distinctive mode of dress, modeled after eighteenth-century Polish noblemen—black, loose-fitting trousers, black leggings, and black silk caftans. Some of the ultra-Orthodox men wear wide-brimmed felt hats over their skullcaps; others dress in black, modern suits and wear black homburgs. On the Sabbath and holidays, many ultra-Orthodox men wear fur hats. The women dress according to the Orthodox norms of female modesty. Married women often cut their hair short or shave their heads altogether and wear wigs. Those who don't wear wigs always have their heads covered with a hat or scarf. You won't see a lot of skin in Jerusalem, and if you are a woman and dress immodestly according to ultra-Orthodox norms, there are areas of the city where you'll have a problem. Bermuda shorts and tank tops will certainly be considered inappropriate, and in some of the ultra-Orthodox areas, a sleeveless dress may provoke disapproving glances, critical remarks, requests to leave the neighborhood, or even stone-throwing.

If you're searching for something to eat in Jerusalem, you won't easily find a cheeseburger, even at an international fast-food chain, nor will you be able to order a milkshake with your hamburger. If you're looking for a movie, pub, restaurant, or disco on Friday night when the Sabbath begins, you can find it, but you have to know where to look. Friday night entertainment is a relatively new, fast-growing phenomenon in Jerusalem, but it's still confined to certain areas. On the Sabbath and Jewish holidays, you'll find that Jerusalem is virtually closed down except for a few isolated commercial centers. The streets are empty, there is no public transportation; and in certain Orthodox areas, the roads are closed to vehicular traffic. A large proportion of the Jewish population is attending one of the 1,000 synagogues, and even those who are not in attendance respect the holy quiet of the city.

Tel Aviv. Tel Aviv, called "the city that never stops," is the secular capital of Israel. It is also Israel's business, cultural, entertainment, and fashion center—the place where you'll find the latest in cinema, theater, and art. Singles and gays view the city as their capital as well. There is not even one Jewish holy site. You'll see far fewer men in skullcaps, and you'll have the feeling that the proportion of modern Orthodox and ultra-Orthodox is much smaller than in Jerusalem. Theirs is not the flavor that dominates. Instead, you'll have the overwhelming sense that you are in a hip, hedonistic, Mediterranean city. Tel Avivians enjoy their outdoor cafes and pubs. Nightlife doesn't really start until 10:00 P.M., and there are traffic jams at two o'clock in the morning. On Friday evenings, everything is open—movie theaters, bars, discos, stand-up comedy, concerts. Although there is no public transportation on the Sabbath, more than 450,000 private vehicles enter the city. You'll see a lot of skin; people tend to dress less modestly than they do in Jerusalem, and many seem to be on the cutting edge of style. If it's hip, unconventional, or avant-garde, you'll find it in Tel Aviv.

3

Second Impressions:
Soldiers, Women, and Israeli Arabs

The first impressions of the sojourner in chapter 2 give rise to three further questions:

Why are there so many soldiers? The large number of soldiers on the streets of Israel—in uniform and carrying weapons—is one of the most disconcerting sights for most Western visitors. In chapter 1, we discussed the importance of the army in Israeli society. The soldiers on the streets serve as a constant reminder of the country's tensions over national security. They also stir Israeli pride in the IDF and "our boys and girls."

Many visitors feel uncomfortable with such a formidable military presence, informal as it may be. Such terms as "armed camp" and "garrison state" have been used by visitors getting acquainted with Israeli culture. The vast majority of Israelis do not feel that way at all. The IDF is basically a civilian army. It consists mainly of young men and women draftees and a large reserve force. There is only a small professional cadre. At any given time, half the total population has served, is presently serving, or will soon serve in the IDF. They and their families, that is, just about everybody, identify strongly with the army. The draft army is composed primarily of "our kids"—eighteen- to twenty-one-year-olds who bear great re-

43

sponsibility and carry commensurate authority while on duty and relax the way young people do while off duty. The soldiers on the street are seen less as an ominous threat than as kids coming home from camp. They may even be treated with indulgence when they exhibit mischievous or scandalously romantic behavior typical of healthy young adults.

Many American visitors are from large cities where very few military uniforms are to be seen at all. Military and naval bases in America are usually located near relatively small towns. There, soldiers and sailors in uniform are familiar. What is probably different in Israel for sojourners from even these locations is that most Israeli soldiers are armed. If a weapon is issued to a soldier, military regulations require that it be in his or her personal possession at all times, together with at least one full ammunition clip.

Another disconcerting sight for Western visitors is women in uniform, especially if they are holding a rifle or submachine gun. Women do not serve in combat, and those women attached to combat units are kept from the front lines of a shooting war. However, many are assigned to bases which are in dangerous areas or must travel through dangerous territory to get to and from their bases. They are expected to protect themselves if the need arises and are thus issued weapons and trained to use them.

There are two types of soldiers in the IDF, identifiable, even for the uninitiated, by their respective uniforms: (a) Soldiers and officers in the regular army—those doing two- or three-year compulsory military service and others who have signed up as officers or for an army career. They wear nicely turned-out uniforms with insignia, ribbons, and patches. (b) Soldiers and officers called up for their two- to four-week annual reserve duty. They wear basic fatigues. The more sophisticated observer, familiar with the color codes of regular army units, can generally identify the type of unit (e.g., air force, infantry, navy, paratroops, armor, engineers) by the various color combinations of boots and berets.

Here are some observations which may prove useful in your encounters with regular or reserve soldiers during your stay in Israel:

- Over time (you may be surprised how short a time), you will probably become accustomed to them. In fact, you will probably learn to become alarmed, as Israelis do, when you don't see any soldiers on the street. That means something serious has happened, and they have all been recalled to base for possible troop deployment.

- While driving the highways or the countryside, you may come across military convoys carrying tanks, mobile artillery, or other tracked armored vehicles. This is seldom a sign of mobilization; instead it usually means that units are being rotated for training or maintenance purposes. Again, what in the U.S. is an unusual scene is in Israel a normal occurrence.

- Many middle- and senior-management personnel in business, government, academia, and other important sectors of Israeli society served as officers when they were in the regular army and continue to serve as officers when they are on reserve duty. Officers may be called for duty for as long as sixty days per year, depending on their rank and type of unit. Although you may find this disconcerting, even frustrating if you need to meet with some specific person, you will discover that in almost all cases, the organization has developed a backup system which assures continuity of assignments and communication.

When they are on reserve duty, many Israelis frequently check in with the office. On their way home on leave, they may drop in at work to say hello to colleagues and generally keep updated on what is going on. It may well happen that while you are sitting in an air-conditioned carpeted office, you will see someone walking by in a dirt-encrusted uniform, carrying a rifle and ammunition clip. No one else in the office indicates that anything is amiss. They'll probably call out greetings and ask about the situation at the visiting reservist's particular front. The soldier in question may even be a member of the team dealing with your particular concern, in which case he will probably sit in on your meeting, in the disconcerting incongruity of a field uniform, contributing his input while his rifle is laid casually on the floor. For Israelis, the transition from civilian to soldier and back again—for themselves as well as colleagues—is quick and practiced, though emotionally wearing.

The presence of so many weapons on the streets, in the hands of both soldiers and civilians, has frequently raised questions about how Israelis settle disputes. You may notice that sound levels on city streets are generally higher than in Western countries. Many of those decibels come from the shouting which occurs in arguments and disputes. Israelis can shout, curse, yell, and argue with the best of other Mediterranean and Middle Eastern peoples. What is sometimes labeled "verbal violence" in the U.S. is a frequent occurrence in Israel. When visitors from the U.S. witness an argument in which verbal violence escalates, they frequently assume that physical violence will follow. It usually doesn't. If it does, spectators often step in to pull the antagonists apart.

There are Israelis involved in violent crime, family violence, and other deviant behaviors. However, Israeli culture as a whole is surprisingly nonviolent, at least so far as use of firearms is concerned. We do not presume to explain a phenomenon of such complexity. The fact is that in Israel, weapons are not used to solve disputes to any statistically significant degree. The occupied territories, which many Israelis refer to by their ancient biblical names—Judea and Samaria—fall into another category. The social history of those areas is not that of Israeli society generally. Since 1967, the IDF has been responsible for maintaining order in the territories because they are under military occupation according to international law. In 1987, the *intifada* broke out. The intifada is the Arabic term for the popular uprising of Palestinian residents of the West Bank and the Gaza Strip against continued Israeli military occupation. It generated both demonstrations and violent incidents within the territories and an increase in terrorist incidents within the green line (pre-1967 armistice lines). It also generated forceful responses from the Israeli army.

As of the publication of this book, there is a question as to whether the intifada should be looked upon as a phenomenon of the past. The 1993 agreement with the PLO called for an end to the intifada and to terrorism. However, some Palestinian political groups have refused to accept the agreement and have encouraged their members, in some cases quite successfully, to continue both the intifada and terrorist activities. Others have accepted the agreement conditionally but have warned that they will return to the intifada and terrorist activity if negotiations about the modalities of Palestinian autonomy reach a dead end or the agreement does not live up to their expectations.

The cycles of violence and counterviolence in the territories seem to have had an impact on social norms in Israeli society. Soldiers returning from the territories sometimes bring their experiences into civilian life. The threshold at which a verbal argument turns into a violent dispute seems to have become lower.

Are women in Israel really as strong, independent, and liberated as they seem? American visitors' initial impressions about the status of Israeli women are usually distinct. There is little in their appearance or demeanor which suggests that Israeli women are, or feel, in any way inferior to men. Women soldiers can be seen everywhere. Some carry guns. There seems to be an easy camaraderie between the sexes. Observing body language—posture, stance, eye contact, gestures—and listening to voice tones even if one cannot understand Hebrew, one gets the impression that Israeli women are as confident and outspoken as Israeli men. Nobody is going to boss them around!

In fact, gender relationships are much more complex than they appear at first glance. To a certain extent, the attitudes and norms of the community in which they were raised are reflected in men and women's behavior, even if they are second- or third-generation Israelis. On the other hand, becoming an Israeli has almost always meant moving in the direction of modern Western, rather than Eastern or Eastern European, norms and attitudes. Daughters of immigrants come to resemble each other much more than they resemble their mothers.

In practical terms, this has usually meant that the longer an immigrant is exposed to Israeli culture, the more difficult it becomes to accept a situation in which women's roles are narrowly circumscribed, women are viewed as inferior, or strict sexual norms are maintained. In this respect, Israel as an immigrant society resembles the United States. In both societies, the cultural pull is in a Western direction. There are important differences, however. Third-, fourth-, and fifth-generation Americans are further removed from their ethnic roots than first- and second-generation Israelis, who may be living in the same home with their immigrant parents or grandparents. Some 50 percent of the Israeli population traces its roots to North Africa and the Middle East. A much smaller proportion of the U.S. population is made up of recent immigrants with non-Western roots. Communities with non-Western traditions are strongly felt ingredients in the Israeli ethnic mix. Their norms and attitudes about the role of women continue to have a direct influence on Israeli behavior.

Male-female relationships, women's legal status, and societal attitudes toward women are also influenced by Jewish religious tradition. The Halakha is the system of Jewish rabbinical law developed and codified by religious scholars over several thousand years. It prescribes separate roles for men and women and is based on the assumption that a woman is the "sanctified property" of her husband. As stated above, the population of Israel runs along the entire religious spectrum from ultra-Orthodox to totally secular. The greater one's Orthodoxy (however one personally defines Orthodoxy), the more likely one is to adhere to the Halakha and to share its basic assumptions about women.

The Halakha has a direct bearing on the legal status of women in Israel. Americans accustomed to the separation between church and state may be surprised to discover that, in Israel, little such separation exists. Instead, Israeli citizens are subject to both civil and religious law. The Israeli Proclamation of Independence guarantees equal social and political rights to all Israeli citizens irrespective of race, religion, or gender. Israeli women are protected by civil laws which grant them the same rights and duties as men, guarantee equality of opportunity, and forbid discrimination in the workplace. However, religious courts, controlled by the Orthodox rabbinate, have exclusive jurisdiction over all matters related to personal status, i.e., marriage and divorce. As there is no civil marriage or divorce, all Israeli Jews, religious and secular alike, are subject to decisions on these issues made according to the Halakha. The Halakha is biased in favor of men: a divorce has to be given by the husband to his wife; a woman remains married unless her husband consents to a divorce; a woman whose husband has disappeared and is presumed, but not proven, dead, is forbidden to remarry; and women are not allowed to give evidence in religious courts.

The degree to which attitudes expressed in the rabbinical courts reflect those of the society as a whole is impossible to estimate with any degree of objectivity. What we do know is that the 1947 decision to allow the Orthodox rabbinical establishment to maintain jurisdiction over all matters concerning personal status reflected political expedience. (See discussion of the status quo on page 39.)

What is one to make of all this ambiguity? Perhaps we should take a look at two institutions—the kibbutz and the army—both of which are sources of the stereotype of the Israeli woman fostered by the media in Israel and abroad.

Kibbutzim are communal agricultural settlements originally established by Israel's founding generation. Although the kibbutzim account for only 3-4 percent of Israel's population, they have always been an intrinsic part of the image of Israel and Israel's image of itself. For many people, the kibbutz is synonymous with the liberated Israeli woman.

Return to the land and hard physical labor in a socialist, egalitarian environment were inherent in early Zionist ideology. In fact, the kibbutz was designed in part to assure sexual equality. Since it was a communal settlement—"from each according to his ability, to each according to his needs"—women were to be freed from traditional roles generally and from economic dependence on their husbands in particular. Children were to be raised in special quarters—children's houses—where they were cared for by nurses and teachers, both male and female. Since cooking, laundering, and sewing were done communally, by rotated assignments, women were to be as free as men to devote themselves to the commune.

Many women in the founding generation did do backbreaking work in the fields, alongside the men. However, as the years went by and the kibbutz as an institution became more established, male-female roles increasingly began to resemble those in society at large. Visitors to kibbutzim today will find most of the men working in agriculture and industry (one would be hard-pressed to discover a woman driving a tractor) and most of the women working in the service branches—the kitchen, laundry, and schools. The division of roles according to sexual stereotypes has undoubtedly developed for a multiplicity of reasons. One reason seems to be that many kibbutz women prefer to be relieved of the backbreaking physical labor that their grandmothers assumed with such ideological zeal.

Another major change, relatively recent, reflects the extent to which life on the kibbutz has veered from its original egalitarian ideology. The separate children's house is becoming an anachronism as more and more kibbutzim vote to replace it with family housing. The impetus for the change has come from the women who want to have a greater voice in raising their children. In practical terms, the transition to family housing means that most kibbutz women now work both inside and outside the home, as do their town and city counterparts, and the nuclear family is as characteristic of the kibbutz as it is of society outside the kibbutz.

In chapter 1, we described the army as the nearly universal Israeli experience, one of the factors in Israeli society that lends cohesion and produces a common culture. Examining the effect of the army on gender relationships also requires taking a closer look at the stereotype of the Israeli female soldier: carrying a machine gun, strong, independent, equal, tough, and sexually liberated, she's ready to march into battle with her male counterpart.

The truth is somewhat different. Although Israel is the only country in the world with compulsory military service for women, approximately 40 percent of women are exempt from army service. They are automatically exempt if they are married or have a child, and religious women may choose not to serve. The Orthodox community regards army service as inappropriate for women. In their view, it places men and women in close physical proximity and encourages loose sexual mores, thereby violating norms of female modesty.

Contrary to the commonly held stereotype, most women who serve in the Israeli army do not have positions equal to men. Basic training lasts three weeks, compared to three months for men. Women are specifically barred from combat roles or any posts that might bring them in or near combat. Although women become officers, officers' training for women is separate from the men's courses. The IDF has no women pilots or brigade commanders. Women do serve as doctors, instructors in service branch schools (including the armored corps), intelligence analysts, lawyers, and administrators. However, the vast majority are clerks, secretaries, teachers, or social workers, occupations generally deemed stereotypically female. They are usually attached to male military units and placed under the command of male officers. Indeed, many Israelis view the army as a bastion of male chauvinism.

"The situation"—living with uncertainty, the constant threat of war and the knowledge that one's father, brother, husband, boyfriend, or buddies may be called into combat—has also had a significant effect on the relationship between men and women. Israelis want to live normal lives. Throughout their history, "the situation" has made that difficult. One way to compensate for the abnormality of the situation is to live as normally as possible in one's personal life. In Israel, a normal personal life usually means being part of a stable family in which role expectations for each sex are clearly defined. Women may work outside the home or have full-time careers, but they expect themselves, and are expected by others, to place a high priority on their roles as wives and mothers. Women are identified with the home, which is viewed as a haven from the tensions of army life, reserve duty, and, too often, combat.

The situation described above has practical implications for American visitors. If you are a middle-class, married American woman who works inside or outside the home, the probability is high that your lifestyle isn't very different from that of your Israeli counterparts. Many of your basic attitudes about gender relationships may also prove similar. And what was once unusual for your parents may now be routine for you. Many Israeli couples, especially those in their twenties and thirties, share household chores like cooking, cleaning, and shopping.

Lifestyles which are alternatives to the traditional nuclear family have been gaining legitimacy in Israel during the past ten years, but they remain exceptions rather than the rule. If you are divorced and/or a single parent in the U.S., you may find that you have fewer counterparts in Israel than you are accustomed to. Divorce in Israel is on the rise, but the rate is lower than in many other Western countries. The current

Israeli divorce rate is 25 percent compared to 50 percent in the U.S. And only 9 percent of Israeli families are single-parent families, compared to 25 percent in the U.S. (1993 U.S. Statistical Abstract based on 1992 population data). The "singles scene" exists mainly in Tel Aviv. The same holds true for the gay and lesbian communities which have publicly presented themselves as alternative lifestyles only within the past few years.

If you are a woman with a career and work full-time, you may find that you have fewer Israeli counterparts. This will be especially true if you are in middle or upper management. In recent years, more Israeli women have entered managerial positions, yet only a handful have risen to middle-to-high management levels. Women comprise only 15 percent of managers in the Israeli economy, and the proportion gets smaller as the levels get higher. At the very top, the proportion of women is only 1 to 3 percent. In the U.S., an estimated 40 percent of executives, managers, and administrators are women.

If you regard yourself as a feminist and expect your Israeli counterparts to share your views, you may be in for a surprise. The overwhelming majority of Israeli women view themselves as modern, Western, and liberated. They do not, however, think of themselves, or wish to be thought of, as feminists. The word brings forth associations of unattractive, strident, unfeminine women marching to the barricades, much as it did in the U.S. during the 1970s. A feminist movement similar to NOW exists in Israel, but it has never enjoyed large-scale support. In a country which has always been preoccupied with issues of life and death, feminism is sometimes viewed as a luxury. Others view it as a threat to the stability and normality of the family. At best, it simply does not occupy a high place on the national list of priorities, including that of most women.

Does this mean that Israeli men and women are insensitive to the issues that are part of the male-female agenda in the

U.S.? Perhaps the best way to answer the question is to report the conclusions of American sojourners once they have had an opportunity to compare their first impressions with personal experiences.

Almost universally, both male and female long-term visitors conclude that Israel is a modern Western country. They also conclude that it is sexist. Can it be both? Yes. That's the nature of Israeli ambiguity. The sense is that Israel is approximately where the United States was fifteen to twenty years ago with respect to attitudes toward women, gender relationships, and women's attitudes toward themselves. The time estimate varies and is complicated by the fact that changes in Israel are occurring at an increasingly faster rate. The Clarence Thomas hearing, for example, not only made front-page headlines in Israel; it also increased public awareness of the issue of sexual harassment. How the fifteen- to twenty-year gap is viewed, and the extent to which it is perceived as troublesome, depends on where one stands on gender issues and the nature of one's experience in the U.S. The gap is usually described in negative terms by professional women who grew up in the U.S., especially those in their late twenties or early thirties, who take their relative equality for granted.

It appears that the difference expresses itself most clearly in responses to behavior both American and Israeli women would label "chauvinist," "sexist," and "sexual harassment," as well as in the definitions of those terms. American sojourners seem to feel that the threshold, or the point at which a woman will say something or make an issue, is higher in Israel than it is in the U.S. Here are a few examples:

- American women have been sensitized for years to scrutinize television and newspaper advertisements for any hint of women being used as sexual objects to sell products. They often find much to criticize in the way women are used in Israeli advertising. Israeli women who are the professional and social counterparts of those same American women often laugh and say, "Yes, it's a little sexist. What's the big deal?" If, however, the ad uses bouncing breasts under T-shirts to sell grapefruit and the accompanying text employs obvious double entendres, Israeli women will be offended (they were) and insist (they did) that the ad be taken off the air (it was).

- Flirtatious behavior in the workplace has come to be viewed by both American women and the U.S. legal system as a form of sexual harassment. Israeli women in the workplace and the army are just beginning to talk openly about sexual harassment and to bring cases to court. Sexual harassment, in the Israeli view, is almost always defined as "laying on of hands," especially on breasts or buttocks, or the hint or clear threat that failure to go along with a male sexual demand will be at the cost of one's job or professional advancement. In Israel, flirting is usually regarded as an enjoyable part of the casual and natural relationship between the sexes, even in the workplace. It is seldom regarded as chauvinist and certainly not as sexual harassment, even if it is accompanied by a friendly nudge or pat on the shoulder.

- Addressing women with terms like "sweetie," "toots," or their equivalent is usually considered inappropriate if not illegal in the U.S. of the 1990s. Israeli women may find the behavior patronizing or annoying; the chances that they will make an issue of it are about even. The probability that the behavior in itself will be viewed as sexual harassment or serve as the basis for a sexual harassment suit is close to zero.

American professional women have developed a marked sensitivity to male assumptions that they will perform certain tasks simply because they are women. These tasks range from serving coffee to taking notes at meetings. Many American women will make a point of reminding their male colleagues that they—the men—are just as capable of serving coffee or taking notes as women are. An increasing number of Israeli women react in a similar fashion. For the most part, however, they either tend not to notice the "Can you get me a cup of coffee?" behavior, or notice it and aren't bothered enough to make an issue of it.

Different thresholds for tolerating sexual harassment, sexism, and male chauvinism as well as differences about the definitions of those terms are parts of a larger issue: cultural differences between Americans and Israelis about male-female relationships. These cultural differences will affect your interactions with Israelis, male and female, as will the array of other differences we address throughout the book.

Where are all the Arabs? I know there are Arabs living in Israel. I am not sure what they look like, or how I would identify them unless they conformed to my stereotypes and appeared either in kaffiyehs and burnoose or in fleeting glimpses of veiled women in beautifully embroidered robes. Of course, I know better. I've seen Arabs interviewed on TV, although I'm not sure whether they're Israeli Arabs or Palestinians from the territories. Many of them appear totally Western. But I don't see them here. At least, I don't think that I see them. Where are they?

A short answer: Many Israeli Arabs are indistinguishable in appearance from other Israelis. You'll see them, but won't necessarily be able to identify them as Arabs. They own small businesses or are employed in the service and agricultural sectors of the economy. They may work as doctors and nurses in Israeli hospitals or attend Israeli universities. However, the vast majority of Arabs are to be found in their own cities, towns, and villages. Most members of the country's minorities live in four main centers: the Galilee (including the city of Nazareth), the Triangle (an area southeast of Haifa), the Negev, and Jerusalem. There are also a small number of urban areas in which Jewish and Arab populations live in their own respective neighborhoods, or even in mixed neighborhoods. These include Acre, Haifa, Lod, Ramla, and Jaffa. The total number of Arabs living in these Jewish towns or cities is approximately 10,000.[1] Even fewer Jews live in Arab towns, cities, or villages.

Arab integration into Israeli professional life is relatively marginal. If you are visiting Israel on a professional assignment, the likelihood that you will encounter an Arab counterpart is small, though the probability varies from profession to profession. Unless you make a special effort to do so, it is unlikely that you will have more than a few chance encounters with Israel's Arab citizens. Though Arabs and Jews live together in Israel, they do not share their day-to-day lives. (It is important to emphasize that our discussion concerns Arab citizens of Israel. We are not describing the situation of Arabs who live in the territories.)

Generally speaking:

- Arabs and Jews do not live in the same towns or neighborhoods.

- Arab and Jewish children do not attend the same schools.

- Arab-owned businesses are not located in shopping districts in Jewish areas, and vice versa.

- Arab professionals are prohibited from working in the military or aerospace industries or in government bodies dealing with those industries.

- Arabs and Jews will not be found in social gatherings in each other's homes.

This situation was not created by the State of Israel. Indeed, ethnoreligious communities in the Middle East have lived separately for centuries. Once a Jewish state was cre-

---

[1] Danny Rabinovitch, "Arabs in Jewish Neighborhoods" (in Hebrew), *HaAretz*, 13 August 1993, 4B.

ated, there was no reason to change this situation, and several reasons to maintain it.

Political borders may change, but cultural patterns linger for generations. Throughout history, Middle Eastern empires were governed through relatively autonomous tribal or ethnoreligious communities. These communities were managed by self-selected (but imperially approved) leaders and were held together by adherence to strict norms and religious traditions.

Individuals and families were members of an ethnoreligious community; they were not independent citizens, partners to a contract with the state. The empire generally recognized the integrity of these ethnic communities. A compact existed: The empire provided protection from foreign invasion, kept the peace among the often fractious subject communities, maintained security of trade routes and currency, and allowed some degree of religious freedom and political autonomy. In return, the subject communities paid taxes (and some well-placed bribes when occasion demanded), refrained from rebellion, and displayed the necessary ritual obeisance to the ruling power.

Under the Ottoman Empire (1517-1917), this pattern of imperial rule came to be called the *millet* system. Each ethnic/religious/national community constituted a millet. As the Ottoman Empire disintegrated, national leaderships emerged in the various millet communities. Jews (especially the European-born Zionists arriving in Palestine during the 1880s), Muslim Arabs, Christian Arabs, and other groups began to develop nationalist ideologies, some more quickly and more comprehensively than others.

The British inherited this situation after World War I when they received the Palestine Mandate from the League of Nations. They changed little, except to clean up much of the corruption. The relations between Jewish and Arab communities in Palestine, never overly friendly, deteriorated as the Zionist movement succeeded in purchasing land (mostly from absentee landlords) and establishing settlements. Armed conflict erupted in 1929 and again in 1936-39. To a considerable extent, the Arab-Jewish conflict was put "on hold" for the duration of the Second World War, as each side devoted its energies to the larger struggle.

As a result of the 1947-1948 war, some 600,000 Palestinian Arabs migrated out of the area which became the new Jewish state. (Some Arab sources place the figure at 700,000. There are no exact figures available and the estimates vary. However, at the time, the official United Nations estimates were just under 500,000.) The majority moved to what is now the West Bank and Jordan, while others moved to the Gaza Strip, Lebanon, and Syria. Many Palestinian Arabs ended up in refugee camps. After the war, 167,000 Arabs remained in Israel or returned under family reunification programs.

Though the withdrawal of British forces marked the end of imperial rule in the region, the millet system's cultural pattern was inherited by the newly created State of Israel. Religious and ethnic communities—Jews, Druze, Bedouin, Muslim, and Christian Arabs—lived separate lives and managed their affairs according to their own norms, rituals, and leadership patterns. Each community lived in its own network of towns and villages.

This situation could not remain static. The millet system worked when the ruling power was distant and neutral. Once one of the subject communities became the ruling power, however, it began to arrogate rights and resources to itself and to allocate them according to its own interests. The Jews had been a minority community under the Ottomans and the British; the various Arab communities had constituted an overwhelming majority. When the State of Israel was established, the Jews became a majority, and the Israeli Arabs became a minority, a situation unfamiliar to both groups.

The new Israeli government imposed a military administration on the Arabs, many of whom had fought against the Jews in the 1947-1948 war. The military administration was not imposed on Druze villages, as they had allied themselves with the Jewish forces. Military rule, which caused many problems for Arab citizens and exacerbated ambivalent attitudes toward the state, was finally lifted in 1966. (Most Israeli Arabs, and in fact many Jews, were surprised that the military administration was not reimposed during the 1967 Six-Day War.) Arab towns and villages then became recognized municipal entities within the civil and legal framework of the state, similar in status to Jewish municipalities.

Legally, Arab citizens of Israel have status equal with Jews. They are entitled to vote, to serve in the national legislature, to sue in court (up to and including the Supreme Court), and to receive all the benefits of the Israeli welfare and educational systems. Nevertheless, Israeli Arabs are pulled in several directions simultaneously.

They are Arabs living in a country defined by the national legislature as the "state of the Jewish people." The Arab population has no reason to share the ideology and national ambitions of the Jewish majority. The Zionist ideology, which they do not share but which is the raison d'être of the country, posits a Jewish state based on *aliyah* (immigration) of Diaspora Jewry to the Jewish homeland.

Israeli Arabs hold Israeli citizenship but most define themselves as Palestinians. They are constantly expected to prove their loyalty to the state. Although the vast majority have shown themselves to be loyal citizens, many Jews do not take their loyalty for granted. Israel has been in a constant state of military and political confrontation with the Arab states and the Palestinians in the occupied territories. Indeed, a vocal minority of Jewish citizens have difficulty accepting the principle of equality for Jews and Arabs. Most Arabs are exempted from compulsory service in the IDF, the stated reason being their family, religious, and cultural affiliations with countries in a state of war with Israel. (Arabs may volunteer for military service, however. Bedouin have served in the army for years, and the numbers are increasing. In recent years, a small minority of several hundred Palestinian Israeli Arabs have volunteered for army service. The IDF accepts only those who pass stringent security checks.) Almost all Israeli Arabs have relatives in the West Bank and Gaza, who, in turn, expect them to show sympathy for, or participate in, the struggle for Palestinian national rights. In addition, most Arabs in the countries surrounding Israel have reservations about Israeli Arabs. They are Arabs, but citizens of a state with which most Arab countries are still at war, or were so until very recently.

Israeli Arabs are thus in an ambiguous situation. A minority in Israeli Jewish society, regarded with ambivalence by the surrounding Arab world, they are constantly struggling to meet contradictory expectations. Over time, that struggle has crystallized into political activism regarding three major issues: working peacefully for the creation of a Palestinian state alongside Israel, dealing with discrimination in Israeli society, and closing the economic gap between Israeli Jewish and Arab populations. The average income for Israeli Arab families is about 50 percent of the average for Jewish families.

To a certain extent, history provides a partial answer to our earlier question about where the Arabs are in Israel and why. Israeli Arabs are not integrated into Israeli life because of inherited patterns of separation of ethnic communities; legitimate differences in language, culture, and religion; social and institutional discrimination; and continued suspicion on the part of both Jews and Arabs regarding the other's peaceful intentions. Animosities accumulated over generations of conflict usually don't disappear overnight, even if the problems that have generated the animosities are resolved. This does not seem likely to occur in the foreseeable future.

In contemporary Israel, it is virtually impossible to discuss the Palestinian issue without entering into passionate, value-laden arguments. Events are too recent, too close to the surface, too raw. Whether the Arabs left by choice in 1947-1948 or were pushed out is a subject of debate among historians. There is probably truth in both positions. Should a massive effort be made to integrate the Arab minority into the Jewish majority, regardless of the conflict between Israel and many of its surrounding hostile neighbors? Again, there are persuasive arguments for each point of view. We invite you to ask questions, hear the arguments, and come to your own conclusions.

4

Coloring Books, Video Recorders, and Sandpaper: Three Cultural Metaphors

In chapter 1, we described Israel as a cultural mosaic. At first glance, the many pieces in the mosaic or puzzle fail to form a discernible pattern; that is, there doesn't seem to be a single homogeneous Israeli culture. Israel is both Western and Eastern, secular and religious.

This difficulty in understanding the nature of Israeli culture is compounded by its kaleidoscopic character. The picture keeps changing. In a developmental analogy, Israel is in its adolescent stage. It is engaged in the process of maturing, of growing to adulthood and creating its own personality. The developmental process is full of energy and action. It is confused and confusing. Little about the society and culture has completely crystallized. Growth spurts occur in several directions at once.

If one studies the puzzle carefully, however, the pieces do fall into place; there *is* a discernible pattern. Certain behaviors, norms, and attitudes are widely shared among Israelis and are encouraged; others are discouraged. It is in the nexus of these shared values and behaviors that the culture of Israel can be found, and that is what we mean by the term "Israeli culture." New immigrants pick up the message quite accurately and quite quickly: there are ways of speaking and

63

acting that are "Israeli." If one wants to be included in the society, those ways of speaking and acting must be incorporated into one's repertoire. If one does not take on those attitudes and behaviors, he or she will be "included out."

Three images serve as metaphors for those behaviors and attitudes which we believe are recognizably Israeli. The images are: a page from a coloring book, the "fast-forward" mode on a video recorder, and sandpaper.

The Coloring Book

Take a close look at the pictures from the coloring book. Picture A is an exact duplication of a page in a children's coloring book. Pictures B and C reflect the perceptions of Americans and Israelis, respectively. "Israelis can't stay within the lines of the coloring book," Americans frequently say. The fact is that Americans and Israelis have different mental images of the same picture in the coloring book. The American mental image of the coloring book often corresponds to drawing B. In the American picture, all of the lines are solid and clearly defined. In the Israeli picture—drawing C—the lines themselves are blurred and even indistinct in places. Whoever has worked on the picture has colored outside the lines. The "artist" was not restrained by the borders, but felt free to create something beyond the defined lines and to make it his or her own. On the other hand, the results give the impression of things being a little out of control. The coloring does not seem to be carefully planned or thought out. The whole picture has an unfinished quality. It may turn out to be a charming example of free-form creativity, or simply a mess.

A: Standard Coloring Book Picture

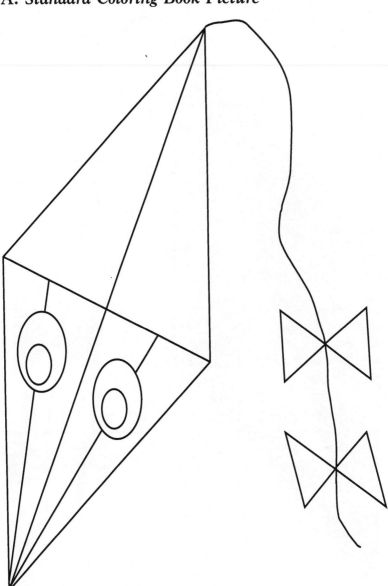

B: *American Perception*

C: *Israeli Perception*

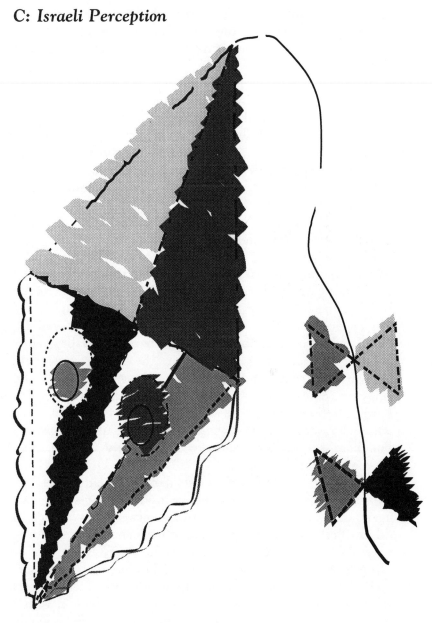

Perhaps the picture in the coloring book also reflects a lack of maturity. After all, growing up usually means accepting restraints on your freedom, the necessity sometimes to color only *inside* the lines.

There is little in their culture which encourages Israelis to stay within the lines in the coloring book. Israelis do not regard staying within the lines as an inherently good thing. Indeed, the lines represent limits to be tested or crossed. Our references to the coloring book in this and subsequent chapters refer to the Israeli perception of the coloring book, i.e., the manner in which Israelis relate to limits, boundaries, and borders.

The coloring book analogy allows us to examine several Israeli cultural characteristics:

Informal patterns of personal interaction. The fuzzy lines which separate the elements in the picture symbolize the informality which distinguishes Israeli society. In a formal society, the differences between groups (social classes, age groups, occupational groups) are marked by explicit symbols, rules, and ritual behaviors. In Israel, where informality has its roots in the socialist egalitarianism of the early settlers, there are very few such symbols, rules, or ritual behaviors. The rules that do exist are often ambiguous. In short, the lines or borders between groups are unclear. Members of groups know who belongs to their group and who belongs to other groups, but there is a stubborn tendency to ignore the boundaries of class and status.

All of this serves to confuse outsiders because the cues they expect are missing. The lines between subordinates and managers are often blurred, as are those between individuals in other roles: parents and children, officers and soldiers, teachers and students, salespeople and customers. To Americans, it often seems as if Israelis are crossing borders that for Americans are quite clear, not fuzzy. The manner in which workers relate to bosses seems insubordinate and the way in which bosses relate to workers seems unprofessional. Salespeople appear to be rude, rather than informal, and the lack of distance between teachers and students or officers and soldiers is viewed as disrespectful rather than relaxed.

A closer look at the picture in the coloring book also reveals that a great deal is unfinished. Everything hasn't been completely filled in. Israeli informality and disregard of ceremony affect outward appearance as well as behavior. A high value is *not* placed on smooth, polished, or finished exteriors. Consider the following scenes:

- You pass by a fancy boutique in a prestigious neighborhood. You are impressed with the window display of the merchandise. Then you discover that the hose from the air conditioner is hanging free over the entrance to the boutique. If you're lucky, the end of the hose is stuck into a soda bottle by the front door and you won't get dripped on as you enter the shop.

- You walk into the office of the marketing manager of a major corporation. The office has wall-to-wall carpeting, teak bookshelves, a large desk, state-of-the-art office equipment. The manager is even wearing a jacket. You are impressed. Then you glance at his desk again. Instead of a box of tissues, there is a roll of toilet paper! Or the socket into which the state-of-the-art equipment is plugged is missing its cover. Or the expensively framed Matisse print is sitting on the floor waiting to be hung.

When it comes to external appearances, Israelis don't deliberately choose the unfinished option. If asked, they won't say that they prefer the air-conditioning hose stuck into the soda bottle. The Israeli eye simply doesn't notice things that, to the American eye, are out of place, jarring, unfinished— out of line.

Improvisational approach to problem solving. The desire to go beyond the limits explains the Israeli improvisational approach to problem solving. Israelis regard the lines of the coloring book as an obstacle to creativity or, from another perspective, as a springboard to improvisation. In the workplace, in particular, the *ability* to improvise as well as the *tendency* to do so expresses itself in every area. Israelis cannot be bothered with "doing it by the book." They prefer to take a system apart, to find new or better ways of achieving a goal or solving a problem. Indeed, it is precisely the Israeli capacity for creativity and the ability to improvise which have for many years attracted clients interested in joint ventures in the area of research and development.

Spontaneity. The Israeli communication style is spontaneous, natural, and unrestrained. In the workplace, spontaneity expresses itself in the ability to come up with on-the-spot solutions to problems instead of relying on the book or being limited by it. Staying within the bounds of expected conduct is confining. In a formal meeting, Israeli representatives may offer their views as they come to mind without considering whether they are interrupting, or whether offering an opinion at a particular juncture is appropriate. From an American perspective, that behavior is out of line, that is, aggressive, if not offensive.

Spontaneity in the workplace sometimes expresses itself in a tendency to "wing it." It is not unusual, for example, to witness a staff presentation which seems extemporaneous. It is obvious that the presenter is well grounded in the material and that the presentation has substance, but it clearly has not been thought out systematically in advance. ("I don't prepare ahead of time because it is too confining," many Israelis say.)

In everyday encounters, the inability to stay within the lines is demonstrated literally. Israelis have difficulty waiting in line at banks, movie theaters, health clinics.... An Israeli line is amorphous. It is often hard to tell where it begins and where it ends. Sometimes it is even hard to figure out who's in front of whom.

Spontaneity expresses itself in social encounters as a lack of inhibition. If you want to invite someone to your home, you do so. If you are interested in how much someone paid for an apartment or dress, you ask. If you are angry, you show it. If you want to give advice, you give it, even if the advice is unsolicited.

Positive attitude toward risk taking. The readiness to color outside the lines means that the individual working on the picture is willing to take a risk. Maybe the picture will be a mess; maybe it won't. In the workplace this attitude expresses itself in a tendency to try out new approaches even if they have not been carefully thought through. All of this produces many surprises; but again, surprises are accepted as normal in Israeli life.

In commercial and bureaucratic encounters, the positive attitude toward risk taking expresses itself in a willingness to test the rules: "It's true that the sign says your office is closed, but I'm going to pretend that it is still open. The worst that can happen is that you'll say no and try to throw me out, but even that is negotiable." (Americans also possess a positive approach to risk taking, but the quality expresses itself differently in the two cultures. See chapter 6 for a discussion of the differences.)

Self-confidence. Israelis are confident that going out of the lines will work, and even if it doesn't work, they are self-confident enough to take the risk. But, as some outsiders have noticed, there is a thin line between self-confidence and arrogance.

Self-confidence expresses itself in the willingness to improvise, to develop creative solutions for problems in the work environment, to question authority, to make decisions outside the boundaries of one's job description, to risk oneself in a sexual or social encounter. Arrogance expresses itself in a haughty attitude toward those who choose to color inside the lines. The implicit message is: people who stay within the lines of the coloring book (e.g., behave solely according to instructions or established procedures), lack self-confidence. They are rigid, afraid to risk, "square."

A combination of informality, spontaneity, a positive attitude toward risk taking, the improvisational approach to problem solving, and self-confidence explains the easygoing Israeli approach toward planning.

The outline of the picture in the coloring book is a framework providing shape and structure, but Israelis do not view themselves as limited by frameworks. Indeed, few Israelis would expect anyone to color inside the lines. The framework of the picture is analogous to a plan.

Army officers and noncoms are taught to plan. They are taught well. At the same time, they are also taught that *a plan is a basis for change*. The message is drummed into their heads: "Don't be controlled by your plan. Use it to respond to the situation in front of you. Be flexible! Improvise." Most Israelis in senior positions in virtually every civilian field are veterans of the IDF officer corps. They bring to their civilian positions the style of responding and approach to planning that they learned during their army service.

The idea of a plan as a basis for change often finds expression in the workplace. Plans, schedules, and deadlines are viewed as broad guidelines subject to alteration; they are not felt to be binding commitments. (A guideline is simply another line in the drawing.)

Leisure-time activities are also affected by the flexible attitude toward plans and planning. A guide in an organized tour may decide to change the plan and alter the itinerary described in the company brochure.

Individualism. Israelis are highly individualistic, as are Americans, but the trait expresses itself differently in the two cultures. The picture in the coloring book helps us understand what individualism means in Israel. One can almost hear the Israeli who colored the picture saying, "No one is going to tell me how to color the picture. I'll do it my way." Israeli individualism expresses itself in a casual attitude toward rules and regulations, a tendency not to follow instructions, and a resistance to imposed authority. ("Do it because

I said so.") Israelis usually have to be convinced that a certain goal should be achieved or a given procedure should be adhered to before they agree to follow orders.

Individualism also expresses itself in self-reliance: "I don't need to ask for help. I can do it myself." Yet Israel's is also a culture in which individualism exists side by side with strong group attachments. Israelis identify themselves as members of groups, are loyal to group members, and are concerned with the well-being and collective interests of the group (e.g., work teams, friendship circles, ethnic organizations, and army units). (See discussion of Israeli group orientation in chapter 8.)

Self-reliance is also a strong component of individualism in American culture. Americans believe, as do Israelis, that individuals should be encouraged to solve their own problems and make their own decisions. In other respects, however, the word carries a different meaning. American individualism is expressed in the pursuit of individual rather than common or collective interests. Americans usually view the world from the point of view of the self. One's loyalty is primarily to oneself and one's immediate family, and attachments to groups are relatively loose. American individualism does not appear to conflict with conformity to regulations, going by the rules, or respect for authority.

Many people would argue that Israelis are changing as the country becomes less socialistic and more capitalistic and that, as a result, Israeli individualism is gradually coming to resemble American individualism. The differences remain marked, however. Perhaps the easiest way to understand them is to look at how each group sees the other's behavior. Americans look at behavior which Israelis call "Israeli individualism" and label it childishness, insubordination, disrespect, anarchy, and arrogance. Israelis look at behavior which Americans call "American individualism" and label it selfishness or egotism.

Limited respect for authority/casual attitude toward rules and regulations. By definition, authority implies the existence of limits and constraints: clearly defined rules concerning what is permissible and what is not. Respect for authority means that one stays within the lines, observes the rules. In the Israeli coloring book, however, the lines are either hard to discern or subject to testing.

In everyday life, behavior in the public parking lot is an example of the casual (some would argue indifferent) Israeli attitude toward rules and regulations as well as evidence of their individualism and their improvisational approach to problem solving. (See illustration on page 75.) Indeed, the arrangement of cars in the parking lot reveals a great deal about Israeli attitudes toward boundaries and border crossings. Painted demarcation lines, denoting parking spaces, are identical to those in parking lots in all Western countries.

In an Israeli parking lot, however, cars may be parked *on* the line instead of *between* the lines; three cars will be crowded into spaces designed for two. Cars may be parked perpendicular to the cars between the lines, or they may be parked on the islands separating the lanes. Cars will not only be parked in ingenious ways, they will also be parked in the space in which the sign clearly proclaims "no parking." (Some people think that the way Israelis park can be explained by the fact that there are too many cars and too few parking lots in Israeli cities. But even when there is plenty of space, the parking-lot picture tends to look the same.)

Somehow, Israelis devise ingenious ways of solving their parking problems, even if doing so means that the overall result is extremely disorderly. In fact, one person's solution to the parking problem may in turn create difficulties for other drivers who discover that it is almost impossible to move into or out of a space, or into or out of the parking lot itself. That becomes a problem-solving challenge for those drivers, often leading to a higher order of ingenuity and improvisation.

If one has parked in a tow-away zone and been graced with

a boot on one's car (Israelis *do* receive parking tickets for violations and *do* pay heavy fines), one feels free to argue with the officer in charge, to "step out of line."

Consider the following scene:

A newcomer to the city is driving on a busy street looking for a place to park. He sees cars parked on the sidewalk or with the side wheels up on the curb. Where he comes from, sidewalks are for pedestrians. Uncertain whether parking on the sidewalk is permissible in Israel, he stops a policeman.

Newcomer: "Is it OK if I park my car on the sidewalk?"
Policeman: "Of course not. It's illegal."
Newcomer: "What about all of these cars?"
Policeman: "Their drivers didn't ask!"

The Fast-Forward Mode
on the Video Cassette Recorder

Our second metaphorical image is the fast-forward mode of a video cassette recorder (see below). On "play," everything is as it should be, moving at a normal pace and rhythm. When one presses the fast-forward button, the pictures on the television screen flash by in rapid succession. It is difficult for the viewer to keep track of the movements of arms, legs, and "talking heads." All the figures appear to be very animated, like characters in a cartoon. Everything is hurried and nothing stays on the screen for more than a moment.

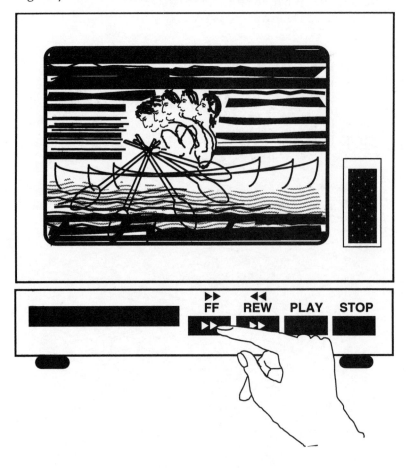

The fast-forward analogy sheds additional light on informality as an Israeli cultural trait. In an informal culture, the transition from stranger to acquaintance occurs at a rapid pace; people get to know each other quickly and feel free to shift into a closer personal relationship at a relatively early point. Since Israeli culture is more informal than American culture, or almost any other, it often seems that Israelis operate on the fast-forward mode while Americans operate on "play."

Fast-forward expresses itself in both business and social settings. An Israeli who is a guest or stranger at a formal meeting in the workplace may behave as if he or she has known the other participants for years. This will usually include shifting into a direct mode of communication at a surprisingly early and, from an American point of view, sometimes inappropriate juncture: "Let's forget all these welcoming speeches and get down to work!"

In social encounters, distances are bridged quickly. There are few social barriers, and those that exist disintegrate rapidly. Israelis feel uncomfortable standing on ceremony. Small talk, for example, may be short-lived or nonexistent. "Hello. Nice to have you as a guest in our home. How was your trip? So you work for the Atomic Energy Commission. How did you ever allow Three-Mile Island to happen?" From the American perspective, all of this occurs in fast-forward. Messages may be garbled, the picture unclear. Indeed, fast-forward often induces sensory and emotional overload. Foreigners feel uneasy as they try to manage, or at least respond properly to, a barrage of demands normally spread over a longer period of time at a more leisurely, controllable pace.

Sandpaper

Our third metaphor—visual, aural, and tactile—is sandpaper. Sandpaper is rough. When two pieces of sandpaper are rubbed together, they cause friction. The sound may be grating, jarring, irritating. If sandpaper gets rubbed on skin, it hurts. But used to smooth out rough surfaces, sandpaper is an essential tool for every carpenter, professional or amateur. It gets the job done. Of course, sandpaper comes in grades, from extra-rough to extra-fine.

Direct Israeli communication style. The direct Israeli communication style, verbal and nonverbal, is analogous to sandpaper. It is often rough, grating, devoid of a smooth finish. To a considerable extent, Israel retains the unpolished communication style of the frontier. In its extra-rough mode, this style is aggressive; in its extra-fine mode, it is simple and straightforward.

Consider the following scenes:

- You are in a crowded shopping mall. People jostle, push, and bump. There is a great deal of physical contact. The friction of contact in passing is considered normal and does not call for an "excuse me."

- You are conducting a workshop. The Israeli participants tell you that they want feedback on their presentations. Translation: "Never mind the compliments. Lay on the criticism and forget the frills."

- You've just presented your point of view on an important and controversial issue. As an American, chances are that you expect to hear disagreement in the form of: "Excuse me, I have a problem with what you've just said." In Israel you are likely to hear, "You're wrong!"

These experiences are upsetting to the uninitiated. They grate on the senses, rub against the grain.

Sandpaper is rough. The opposite of rough, of course, is smooth. In more formal cultures, high priority is given to teaching children manners—the norms of acceptable speech and behavior. These are viewed as the lubricating niceties that facilitate social interactions. "Lucy, Lucy, if you're able, take your elbows off the table." By the age of seven, children have learned the magic words: please, thank you, excuse me, and such basic formulas as "Mom, this is my friend David. David, I would like you to meet my mom."

Many Americans are convinced that Israelis *never* say please, thank you, or excuse me. The truth is that Israelis do use these polite forms. They are employed much less frequently, however; and Americans, who are accustomed to using and hearing a greater number of them, come away convinced that the words have not been uttered at all!

In many cultures, this kind of rough behavior is avoided at all costs. Filipinos, for instance, place an overriding importance on what is universally called "smooth interpersonal relations." In informal Israel, "smooth" is often suspect. It is equated with being artificial, insincere, hypocritical. Rough is real; it is honest, authentic. Rough hurts, but in Israel, it is assumed that you are able to "dish it out and take it too." Rough works.

Americans will frequently use the phrase: "I'm going to tell you the unvarnished truth" when they are about to communicate something potentially painful. Most do-it-yourselfers know that varnish is put on wood that has already been sandpapered. Wood that is unvarnished is simply unpolished. The American unvarnished truth is considerably smoother than Israeli truth delivered sandpaper style.

If asked (and they have been), Israelis overwhelmingly express preference for directness, however painful, over indirection—messages padded for politeness' sake.

The direct, confrontational, no-frills style is known as "dugri talk" in Israeli slang. The word *dugri* comes from the Arabic where it has a similar, but not identical meaning. The dugri style of speaking characterizes sabra communication style. Part of being an Israeli is "speaking dugri." Dugri, in the minds of many Israelis, is contrasted with more diplomatic, less direct, less confrontational communication styles, which are often perceived by Israelis as insincere and artificial.

Dugri speech, on the other hand, is equated with sincerity and integrity.[1]

In this chapter our discussion has been associative and impressionistic. In the following chapters we will present a systematic analysis of the cultural differences most likely to cause misunderstandings in interactions between Americans and Israelis.

---

[1] For a fascinating discussion of dugri speech, see Tamar Katriel, *Talking Straight: Dugri Speech in Israeli Sabra Culture*. Cambridge: Cambridge University Press, 1986.

Part II

American Encounters with Israelis: Dealing with Different Norms, Expectations, and Behavior Patterns

Same Behavior/Separate Labels: The Differences at a Glance

One way to look at cultural differences is to examine mutual perceptions. Israelis view their behavior one way. Americans see that same behavior and sometimes label it differently. The reverse, of course, is also true.

The following chart[1] provides an overview of American-Israeli cultural differences as they manifest themselves in commercial, bureaucratic, work, and social settings. Please note that neither all Israelis nor all Americans perceive themselves or each other simply in terms of the descriptions included in this chart. Similarly, the way Israelis and Americans perceive and react to each other in any given instance will vary substantially from the categories used here. In fact, Americans and Israelis don't always perceive themselves differently from the way others see them. We know that Freud himself said, "sometimes a cigar is just a cigar." American politeness is often perceived by Israelis as just that—politeness—and is appreciated as such. Likewise, Israeli directness

---

[1] Both parts of the chart represent an expanded version of material designed by Lucy Shahar for cross-cultural workshops.

is often perceived by Americans as just that—directness—and it is viewed positively.

Many Americans and Israelis perceive similarities in each other's speech and behavior. When misunderstandings and conflicts *do* arise, however, they often stem from the differences highlighted in the chart. It is offered as a hypothetical framework for better understanding the cultural differences between Americans and Israelis. The chart is based on fifteen years of professional experience and has been confirmed by the reactions of American and Israeli participants in cross-cultural workshops. The challenge for you is to determine whether our hypotheses are borne out by your experience.

1: Israelis

Israelis tend to see themselves as:	Americans often see Israelis as:
informal	rude, familiar, inconsiderate, disrespectful, insubordinate, unprofessional
outspoken, direct, honest	tactless, rude, blunt, disrespectful, aggressive, stubborn, insubordinate
spontaneous, open, natural	out of control, intrusive, ill-mannered, unprofessional
hospitable, warm	smothering, intrusive, dominating
assertive	aggressive, arrogant, ruthless, stubborn
flexible about plans and schedules; casual about rules and regulations	inefficient, sloppy, unprofessional, undisciplined, arrogant, irresponsible, inconsiderate
creative, able to improvise	superficial, chaotic, undisciplined, unsystematic
active, taking initiative	insubordinate, pushy, undisciplined, intrusive, dominating, aggressive
self-confident	arrogant
willing to take risks	irresponsible, overconfident
wary, alert, realistic	cynical, distrustful

2: Americans

Americans tend to see themselves as:	Israelis often see Americans as:
polite	insincere, artificial, lacking spontaneity, excessively formal
friendly	naive, superficial, sexually provocative, artificial
respectful of privacy (theirs and yours)	distant, unfriendly, lacking spontaneity, shy, excessively formal
sharing personal concerns	tastelessly exposing private matters, unnecessarily revealing, intrusive
organized	rigid, "square," inflexible, efficient at the expense of personal relationships, going by the book instead of improvising, focused on procedures instead of the task at hand
respectful of authority	passive, conforming, excessively formal, excessively mindful of hierarchy, focused on roles rather than goals, *freier* (pronounced "fryer," Hebrew slang for "sucker" or "pushover")
professional	arbitrarily differentiating between work and social spheres, excessively formal
efficient	arbitrarily differentiating between work and social spheres, unfriendly, overly programmed, lacking spontaneity
trusting and trustworthy	naive

5

American Facade/Middle Eastern Behavior: Commercial Transactions and Bureaucratic Encounters

If you are in Israel for an initial visit, your first encounters with Israelis will probably be in everyday commercial transactions and bureaucratic encounters. However, if you are going to be involved with Israelis in the workplace, or if you hope to get to know them through social interactions, those first, seemingly trivial encounters can serve as a means to understand and deal with more significant situations. Several issues we discuss in this setting, e.g., distance and deference, are also sources of misunderstanding in the work and social environments. In this chapter, we'll see how friendliness carries different meanings for Americans and Israelis. In short, whatever is true about a culture will express itself in every area of life. If Israelis "let it all hang out" in their dealings with customers, they are likely to act in a similar way when they deal with their colleagues or when they invite guests to their homes. Those first encounters can serve as your laboratory, allowing you to look at everyday interactions from a different cultural perspective. In the following letter, an American diplomat describes her initial reactions to an Israeli supermarket. We will call her description a "critical incident."

Dear Ann,

I hope that you're saving my letters, because they're going to make a good story—"Joan's Adjustment to the Holy Land." It's very strange—I never thought of myself as a typical spoiled American. I've lived in other cultures. Two years in the Peace Corps and a year in Chile at the American School must count for something! Yet, I'm having more trouble adjusting to Israel than I ever anticipated. (Look at my letters. They show a steady decline). The honeymoon is definitely over. Now that I'm working, I have less time for touring. Instead, I'm involved with the hassles (and I do mean *hassles*) of everyday life, or should I say, the Darwinian struggle for survival.

I know that if you read the word "supermarket," you think "modern." So did I. The new supermarket in my Tel Aviv neighborhood is as well-equipped as any American market, and it's a far cry from the poorly equipped supermarkets in Santiago or the village store in the Indonesian village where we stayed as Peace Corps volunteers. It's shiny, big, and attractive. But the people who work there are something else! I've been using the supermarket for several weeks, so what I'm about to describe is not the result of a one-time-only observation....

Most of the workers at the checkout counter are young or middle-aged women. Their behavior toward me and many other customers, including Israelis, would get them fired from most U.S. markets (and it should!). I know, I know, I sound very obnoxious.

When I reach the checkout counter, the scenario is as follows: The cashier starts processing my purchases and entering the code into the very modern computerized scanner. No smile. No hello. She doesn't even look at me. When it's time for me to pay, I have trouble figuring out the money, and her impatience becomes evident. Once, she even said "Nu?" (the Israeli expression of impatience) and reached into my change purse to take out the right coins. When she gives me my change, she throws it on the counter, even though I have my hand out for the money. Apparently, she's doing me a favor by waiting on me.

The other day, I paid the bill with my credit card. I assumed that she understood that I wanted to make three payments, like everyone else. (Supermarkets often attract customers by enabling them to pay their food bills in a number of interest-free installments.) She punched in the purchase as one installment and when I questioned her, she said, "Why didn't you tell me before I rang it up?" I felt strangely on the defensive. Do you believe this? Yesterday, I couldn't contain myself any longer. I said, "You know, you could say thank you when you take my money or my charge card." She looked at me and replied, clearly very bewildered, "Why should I thank you? It's not my store."

As if all of this weren't puzzling enough, the same cashier seems to be in different moods on different days. Sometimes she smiles, makes eye contact, even exchanges a few pleasantries. At other times, she is rude and unpleasant to practically everyone. Her behavior can change within the space of a few minutes. Yesterday, the cashier who is always incredibly rude to me, and often rude and unpleasant to the other customers, seemed to change her mood in midstream. She smiled pleasantly at a customer she apparently knew, asked her how she and her family were doing, commented on how beautiful her little boy was, and even gave him a piece of candy. In fact, now that I think about it, she plays favorites all the time. Another time, when I was the only other person in line, she got into a long conversation with the man in front of me. From what I could gather, their kids go to the same school. After five minutes, I snapped: "Maybe you could finish your conversation another time." She did stop, but there was no "excuse me." What does she think this is, a social hour?

HELP! I'm not sure I'm going to make it....

Yours,

Joan

Joan comments that the "honeymoon is over" and that her letters show "a steady decline." She is involved in the "hassles of everyday life." Her initial enthusiasm has diminished, as has her expectation that the adjustment to this seemingly Western culture will be relatively easy. Joan's behavior has met with unexpected results, and other people's behavior does not seem to make any sense. In the description of her supermarket encounter, we can sense her vulnerability and frustration. She has not yet developed new skills for coping and communicating. As a result, she is irritable and easily frustrated. Joan is in the process of developing a distinctly negative stereotype of Israelis.

Since she is an experienced sojourner, Joan probably knows, at least on a cognitive level, that she is going through the predictable ups and downs of the cross-cultural adjustment process. She may even be aware that she is undergoing a form of culture shock. She may be less aware, however, of the extent to which the adjustment process is influencing her perceptions. Perhaps the cashier is not "incredibly rude," simply indifferent. Perhaps she places the change on the counter and does not "throw it." (Most cashiers in Israel place your change on the counter, not in your hand; this is often a minor, though persistent, irritant to American visitors.) Perhaps the "long conversation" with another customer merely involved the exchange of a few words. Perhaps she did not hear the clerk's hello if and when it was uttered. And perhaps, to some extent, she is right. She can't be wrong about everything all the time!

Selective perception, which characterizes the early stages of culture shock, explains some of the emotion in Joan's description. But it fails to provide a sufficient explanation for Joan's reaction to the clerk's behavior. Her adventures in the supermarket reflect the sense of frustration and disorientation many Americans experience during their initial commercial encounters in Israel. Her letter could just as easily have described an incident in a restaurant, boutique, gas station, or shopping center. That's why it provides us with an excellent entree into examining some of the cultural differences that reveal themselves in seemingly trivial situations.

American Expectations

If Joan had been buying bread and other daily necessities in a remote village in Indonesia, she would have logically expected the vendor to act differently from a cashier in an American supermarket. Indeed, it is reasonable to assume that her attitude toward delays, differences in personal distance, and the preference for social interactions over efficiency would have been more tolerant. In the Israeli supermarket, however, Joan entered a situation in which the facade, i.e., the physical setting, was familiar, virtually identical, to that of an American supermarket. The physical similarity made it easy for her to assume that the staff's behavior would be similar as well.

Let's take a look at some of the many ways in which the clerk's behavior ran counter to Joan's expectations.

Clearly, service, in Joan's mind, included elements she would define as common courtesy: acknowledgment of her presence via eye contact, a word of greeting, a polite goodbye. In this respect, Joan's expectations were not very different from those of a British, French, or Italian customer. We would argue, however, that as an American, Joan expected more than mere courtesy. She was conditioned to expect friendliness. Indeed, in this situation, Joan viewed friendliness as a component of courtesy. It might not even be an exaggeration to say that friendliness would be part of the cashier's job description if she were working in an American supermarket. It would include, at the very least, a smile, appropriate body language, and a readiness to exchange a few conversational pleasantries.

Joan also expected an individual *in the role of cashier* to defer to her *in the role of customer*. ("The customer is always right.") When she criticized the cashier for carrying on a conversation instead of waiting on her, Joan expected an apology. When the cashier stopped the conversation, but failed to acknowledge her error, she reinforced Joan's impression that she was surly and rude. As far as Joan was concerned, the cashier was not making any effort to please her as a customer. The same cashier added insult to injury by making no attempt to hide her impatience when Joan was having trouble figuring out the currency, and she had the audacity to argue about the credit card payment and blame Joan for the error.

Like many Americans, Joan expected the cashier, *in the role of an employee providing service*, to act the same way toward all customers. Instead, she "played favorites." It is reasonable to assume that this behavior offended Joan's sense of fairness; indeed, fairness seems to be synonymous with uniformity of behavior.

Joan also reported on differences in the cashier's mood and demeanor on different days. She was put off by the lack of predictability, the seemingly arbitrary manner in which whatever was happening in the cashier's life affected the way she related to customers. Joan's implicit assumption seemed to be that a cashier leaving for work in the morning should put on her work face and assume a work personality. Her personal life should have no effect on her behavior in the workplace.

According to Joan's account, the cashier's efficiency varied from day to day. When there were a number of people in line, she processed all the customers so quickly that she did not have time (or did not care) to observe the most elementary rules of courtesy. And then, when there were fewer people in line, the cashier felt free to engage a customer in a five-minute conversation. Joan was annoyed not only by what she termed "favoritism," but also by the fact that the cashier was wasting her (Joan's) time. The cashier's job, in Joan's view, was to process the customers as efficiently as possible, even at the expense of unnecessary social interactions based on off-the-job relationships. Efficiency need not come at the expense of politeness or friendliness. The cashier could process customers at the same time as she was smiling and engaging them in a few pleasantries, just as Joan remembered cashiers doing in the U.S.

When the cashier reached into Joan's purse to take out the right coins, she was invading Joan's private space, defined in American terms as her body and/or her personal possessions. She was violating a nonverbal taboo even though she didn't actually touch Joan. It is safe to assume that Joan expected the cashier to point out the appropriate coins or to ask her to spread the coins on the counter. If the cashier felt it necessary to touch Joan or her possessions, she would, of course, have to ask permission to do so.

Israeli Expectations

It is tempting to sum up the analysis of the Israeli cashier's behavior by saying: "Israelis are just rude, and that's it." After all, rudeness is a critical component of outsiders' stereotypes of the Israeli. Indeed, elements of the cashier's behavior, e.g., indifference and lack of patience, are subjected to daily criticism in the Israeli press. Israeli comedians satirize the tendency to argue, to put the customer on the defensive. They target the lack of a service mentality—the absence of the attitude that the customer is always right.

Our task, however, is to move beyond labels and simplistic explanations. As a first step in our cross-cultural analysis, it might be fruitful to ask ourselves which elements of the clerk's behavior would annoy the Israeli consumer as well, and which would not.

Israelis would be annoyed if there were a long line and the cashier spent five minutes talking to one customer. If the cashier were incompetent, e.g., could not operate the computerized cash register, they would lose patience. A "Nu?" might give rise to annoyance. Lack of eye contact, on the other hand, would most likely escape everyone's notice. The Israelis would *not* be offended by the absence of a smile, a hello, or a thank you, although they would be pleased if they were offered and seemed sincere.

Assuming that there were no grounds to suspect dishonesty, the Israelis would have no objection to the clerk's reaching into their wallet in order to help sort out the change. Israelis certainly would not expect the clerk to ask for permission to do so. It would not be regarded as a violation of personal space. Israelis encountering the same hello, smile, or thank you offered to every customer would be amused or even insulted and might tell the story at the dinner table. It would probably be accompanied by the comment: "We're getting to be too much like America."

The following paragraphs are translated from Hebrew and excerpted from an article that appeared in *HaAretz*, a prestigious daily newspaper. It gives us the Israeli view of a clerk's behavior in an American supermarket. The writer is Uzi Benziman, who was the paper's correspondent in Washington, D.C., during the early 1980s.

When you are exactly thirty centimeters from the cashier at the checkout counter, she smiles and says, "How are you today?" "Fine, thanks," you reply. "Good," she says, as she begins to place your purchases along the moving counter. She processes everything with skill and speed. Via her fast-moving hands, the products pass under the electronic eye of the computerized scanner which records brand names, weights and prices, into double-strength paper bags, and finally into the shopping cart.

A young man stands at the door of the supermarket. When you are exactly thirty centimeters away, he says, "How are you today?" and you answer, "Fine, thanks." He replies, "Good," and helps you load the bags into your car. In the meantime, another customer arrives thirty centimeters from the cashier and she says, "How are you today?" and he answers, "Fine, thanks," and she says, "Good," and starts to register his purchases on the computerized cash register.

The cashier is also computerized. Her voice is that of a computer. She is efficient and exact like a computer. She lacks feelings, just as a computer lacks feelings. You can be a customer at the same supermarket for three years and shop there twice a week, but she will react exactly the same way each time—just like a computer. No extra word, no sign of personal recognition. Until noon, she will say, as you leave, "Have a nice morning!" After twelve noon, she'll say to you, "Have a nice evening." Late in the week, she'll begin saying, "Have a nice weekend." She doesn't recognize you even though you're a regular customer. You always have to present your personal identification. She doesn't distinguish between regular customers and newcomers. As soon as they are thirty centimeters from her, she says to each customer, "How are you today?" and everyone replies according to the agreed-upon text.[1]

Israeli consumers' expectations about service have far-reaching implications for Israeli-American interactions outside of Israel. Engineers sent to the U.S. to provide customer service to American clients have all been clients themselves in Israel. Unless they have received predeparture training which focuses on customer expectations in the American environment (and increasingly they are), they will expect their clients to have the same expectations about service as do their clients in Israel, and they will relate to them in that way.

Israeli customers buying a new refrigerator or television would expect to be sold service. Service would be defined as a year's guarantee and the promise to repair or replace the product if it were defective. They would be pleased if the service were prompt and efficient. Indeed, a firm's record of prompt service would most likely influence their decision to buy the product from that company, and they might even

---

[1] Uzi Benziman, "Discovering America: Modern Times" (in Hebrew), *HaAretz*, 3 June 1984. (Translated by Lucy Shahar.)

recommend the company to their friends. Once the repair-man was working on the appliance, the Israeli customer's major concern (perhaps the only concern) would be the bottom line: can he fix it, how long will it take, and how much is it going to cost? In the final analysis, the criterion for service would be practical in the extreme: "The refrigerator didn't work. It works now. So what if the repairman was a little rude! The guy didn't give up. He worked on the damn thing until it was fixed."

The major difference between an Israeli and American customer lies in the area of expectations. Israeli supermarket customers are not conditioned to expect to be sold service. They expect to be sold milk, eggs, etc. They may move to a competing supermarket if the prices are lower or if the super-market does not meet minimal standards of cleanliness; it is unlikely that they would move to the competition because of the behavior of the employees.

In short, many Israeli businesses are not yet at the eco-nomic stage where consumer awareness compels them to sell service in the form of a polite attitude. Customer service at the Israeli phone company, on the other hand, reflects the Israeli economy in rapid transition. Workers are trained to answer calls by saying, "Hello. This is Ruth. How can I help you?" Their service to the Israeli consumer now includes a polite greeting and an initially deferential attitude to every caller. Surprised, pleased, but somewhat puzzled by the phone company's new approach to service, many consumers' first response is, "Do I know you?"

How we display our public and private selves is also an issue here. Americans expect individuals to exhibit different behav-iors in different roles. Part of the ritual of leaving the house in the morning includes putting on your work face. If you are worried about meeting your mortgage payments or you have just had a fight with your boyfriend, you are expected to leave it all behind. In short, you are supposed to compartmentalize your personality and your life in order to function efficiently and professionally in the work environment.

The Concentric-Circles Analogy

Many Israelis find uniform behavior incomprehensible. There is every reason in the world for people to act warmer toward someone they know than toward a stranger. This attitude becomes understandable if we think of relationships in terms of concentric circles (see page 98).

Care must be taken not to reduce the concentric-circles analogy to a rigid formula or an exotic, folkloric conception of Israeli culture. To a certain extent, the analogy fits virtually all societies, including the U.S. In social situations, for example, American and Israeli behaviors are similar. Strangers are treated differently from acquaintances, and acquaintances are treated differently from friends and family. (The American inclination to be open and friendly to strangers and acquaintances tends to muddy the waters here. But the fact that this behavior confuses Israelis, who expect the friendliness to grow into friendship and are disappointed when it doesn't, indicates that Americans adhere to the concentric-circles analogy in more ways than meet the eye.)

The way Israelis relate to each other is a function of how close one is to the center of another's circles. In different settings, however, concentric-circles behavior is expressed in very different ways. Americans have isolated certain domains in which the concentric-circles pattern of behavior is almost neutralized. This is true in the work environment, and it is especially evident in commercial interactions. In the American environment, the "change in role, change in demeanor" norm tends to be accepted. Americans are trained to provide fair and uniform service to all customers, and customers learn to expect fair and uniform treatment, even if they are friends or family members. In Israel, there is little such training, formal or otherwise, and it is therefore accepted that people relate to others on a personal basis, even in a commercial or business interaction.

The Concentric-Circles Analogy

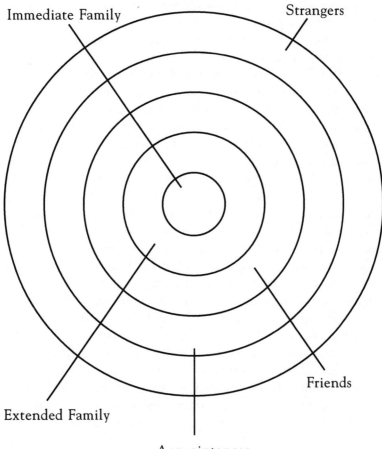

Immediate Family

Strangers

Extended Family

Acquaintances

Friends

Israelis tend *not* to isolate the work domain or assume a different demeanor when they enter the work environment. The borders between work and private life often go outside the lines. Efforts to isolate domains and adopt particular role behaviors seem to characterize Western, large-scale, free-market enterprises. Small towns and small businesses in the U.S. still maintain cultural norms and behaviors reflected in the concentric-circles analogy. It is interesting to note that Americans who come from small towns, or those who have functioned in a small business environment, tend to feel more comfortable and at home in Israeli culture than do their "big city cousins."

The concentric-circles analogy is thus a helpful tool for understanding Israeli behavior in commercial settings; it is *not* a helpful tool for understanding Americans in most commercial settings because Americans tend to "switch off" this pattern of behavior.

The concentric-circles model has clear practical implications. When I, as an American, move closer to the center, e.g., from "stranger" to "acquaintance," the Israeli clerk is likely to transform herself into a warmer, friendlier, more helpful individual. If I left behind six containers of yogurt after I paid for them and then remember them a day later, she is likely to tell me that she returned the yogurt to the refrigerator section and that I should just go ahead and choose six fresh ones. It means that she may leave her position at the cash register (with seven other people in line) in order to help me find something on the shelves. She may express concern if I appear to be under the weather, and it is very likely that I will be greeted with a genuine smile. (Newcomers who get "hooked on Israel" frequently cite this behavior as a major reason. What was first viewed as impersonal or unfair becomes something personal and special.)

Adapting to the Situation

At this point, chances are you're asking yourself: *What should I do when I'm in the supermarket, or bank, or...?* In Appendix A, we address the problem in detail; that is, we discuss the range of coping strategies that are appropriate and effective in Israel. By doing the suggested exercises, you have an opportunity to consider various options and to choose the strategies most consistent with your personal style. At this juncture, however, we would like to offer a few general suggestions:

- When you find yourself in a situation similar to that in the supermarket, remember that you have choices. Ask yourself the following question: Do I care enough to try to change the situation in which I feel uncomfortable?

If the answer is no, the reason may be that you have simply told yourself: "That's how it is here. I am *not* in the U.S. even though the supermarket (or bank or...) facade is identical. I accept things the way they are." Or: "I'd like the clerk to act differently and/or I'd like to be in a supermarket where the behavior of the workers meets my expectations as an American consumer, but I haven't the time or energy to deal with this."

The obvious result: You shrug or laugh and move on to more important things. (This is a perfectly legitimate response; indeed, it is probably the most common form of adaptation to a new culture.)

If the answer is, "Yes, I do care enough to change the situation so that I will feel more comfortable," then here are some options or questions you can ask:

- "Where can I shop where the behavior of the salespeople more closely resembles that in an American supermarket?" In this case, you find a different environment where you do not have to alter *your* behavior.

- Which of my old coping strategies (from the U.S.) will also be effective here? In many situations, it's very possible that you can get along well without changing the way you usually act in day-to-day commercial transactions. You may decide, for example, that it is a violation of your integrity to try to ingratiate yourself with clerks and penetrate the rings of concentric circles in order to get better service. You are more comfortable remaining in the role of customer—complaining to the manager about poor service or offering suggestions.

- How can I alter my behavior in the situation in order to penetrate the concentric circles, i.e., change my status from anonymous stranger to acquaintance or friend? It is likely that newcomers who want to adapt to the culture will answer these questions differently on different occasions. It may be important in the bank, for example, to think about the concentric-circles analogy and act accordingly. The bank clerk, who, at the moment, is not particularly helpful, may possess information that you sorely need. In short, choose your battles.

- To what extent can I change my basic attitude? Am I ready to blur the lines—to regard what is happening as an interaction between two human beings instead of an interaction between a person in the role of customer and someone else in the role of salesperson? The greater the extent to which I am able to do this, the more I become capable of responding like an Israeli.

In order to broaden our understanding of what is likely to occur in everyday commercial transactions, let's look at another incident.

The Garage

An American on an extended assignment in Israel describes the following encounter:

I brought my car into the garage for repair at 10:00 on a weekday morning. The garage was clearly open for business, but none of the workers were around. I asked the secretary where everyone was, and she said that they were all inside on their coffee break. It would be over at 10:30 and then someone would take care of my car. I laughed and said, "This doesn't make any sense. Wouldn't it be more efficient if they went on their break in shifts?" The secretary, who is a bright lady and the daughter of the owner, said, "Sam, you're the fifth American who's asked me that. They'd never agree to go on their break in shifts. What's the point of having a break if you can't sit around and talk to your friends?"

Many garages and other businesses in Israel operate like their counterparts in the United States. Employees go on their breaks in shifts, and managers organize the work schedules in order to maximize productivity and efficiency.

It is also true that the scene the American described above occurs with considerable frequency. Israelis, and those Americans who have been in the country long enough to understand the rules of the game, are careful not to come into garages, service centers, or privately owned workshops when workers go on their half-hour break. Efficiency is not always the highest priority in the workplace. Sometimes maintaining social connections is equally important. American customers are sometimes amused, and very often annoyed, by what they view as an inappropriate use of time.

Another explanation for the employees' behavior is the absence of clear boundaries between work and social roles. This is an extension of the private- versus public-self issue discussed above. The boundary between activities appropriate in the workplace and those appropriate at home is blurred.

Adapting to the Situation

Once again, ask yourself: Do I care enough to try to change the situation?

If the answer is no, shrug and sit and wait patiently (or impatiently) for the end of the coffee break. Remind yourself that next time, it might be a good idea to bring a book or newspaper. You can spend your time productively while the garage workers are engaged in an activity you find unproductive or inappropriate in a work setting.

Or, you can experiment—see how it feels to operate according to a different set of priorities. Start out with the expectation that no work is going to get done until the coffee break is over. Try to penetrate the concentric circles. Ask for a cup of coffee and just relax. Do not try to do anything productive. You might even attempt to join the workers in the room where they are socializing.

A word of caution: In a garage setting, this strategy works better for men, and it doesn't always work even for them. You have to be a regular customer, and you have to feel comfortable with the workers. If they sense that you are coming in to get a bit of local color and to see how the "natives" behave, forget it. Or, if you give the workers the feeling that you are doing a "one-of-the-guys" routine, i.e., you are manipulating them in order to get better or faster work on your car, your behavior will boomerang.

If your answer is that you want to change the situation, think of the alternatives before reacting emotionally. Decide whether to stay with this garage or go elsewhere. There are garages where you will be processed as soon as you come in. But efficiency, almost by definition, is impersonal. Therefore, you have to weigh the trade-offs. The mechanic in the company garage would be less likely to stay after hours to complete a repair on your car or deal with your emergency, even if you were a regular customer, than would his counterpart in a small, privately owned shop.

If you decide to stay with the small, privately owned garage, there are ways in which you can develop additional strategies for penetrating the concentric circles. This will result in a greater chance (no guarantees in the Middle East!)

that one of the workers will sacrifice his coffee break in order to help you. Or you may simply develop some interesting new relationships.

Here's another incident that underlines the importance of the human connection.

Unexpected Difficulties

George, an American immigrant, is a department head in a major social service agency. He relates the following episode:

Shortly after immigrating to Israel, I obtained a job at a social service agency. The position was almost identical to my former job in the U.S. Since I knew Hebrew before I came to Israel, I anticipated very few obstacles in adjusting to the work situation. I thought that I would simply pick up where I had left off. My normal work day, as it had been in the States, began with my grabbing a cup of coffee as soon as I arrived at the office, taking it to my desk, and beginning to work. My colleagues accepted me graciously, but after a few weeks, I discovered that they as well as my subordinates were beginning to regard me strangely. I started to feel uncomfortable. More specifically, I felt left out and I couldn't pinpoint what it was that I was being left out of.

One day, after I had been out of the office for a three-day site visit, I went for my morning cup of coffee. By chance, several of my colleagues were getting their coffee at the same time. It was at the coffee area that I began to catch up on everything that had happened at the office while I was gone. I discovered what had been missing for me: the human connection, or daily reconnection, with the other workers on the staff.

Instead of rushing to put my nose to the grindstone each morning, I got into the habit of taking my cup of coffee on the rounds to my coworkers' desks. We chatted and brought each other up to date on both personal and work-related matters. I felt better, more accepted, and I got the distinct impression that my behavior helped my colleagues and subordinates feel more comfortable with me. I began scheduling the half-hour needed for this activity into my daily calendar.

In collegial relationships, just as in customer-employee relationships, social interactions sometimes take precedence over efficiency. If you are a colleague, instead of (or in addition to being) a customer, you may be amazed to find that your "nose to the grindstone" work style creates tensions with your coworkers.

Find a way to combine the American need to plan and to achieve maximum efficiency with the Israeli (Middle Eastern) concern for maintaining social relationships. Schedule time for social interaction in the workplace. You are likely to discover that playing this new role can produce a change. You may become involved in your coworkers' lives and allow boundaries separating work and private life to blur. You may be expected to attend coworkers' family celebrations. You can also expect late-evening calls at home from subordinates or colleagues who have returned to the office to finish a report if they have questions that require immediate answers.

This concern for tending to relationships in the workplace sometimes causes Americans to reach the conclusion that Israelis lack a work ethic, but Israelis often arrive at similar conclusions about Americans. This strange mutual misunderstanding can be explained in part by the way that people in the two cultures compartmentalize their work and social time. Because social interactions sometimes take precedence over efficiency during traditional work hours, Israelis are frequently perceived as lacking a work ethic. On the other hand, Israelis have trouble understanding why Americans are annoyed when they are called at home to discuss a work-related issue, or why Americans "drop their pencils" at 5:00 P.M. Work is just as likely to infringe on personal time as social interaction is to occur during work time. (Additional cultural differences in work style are discussed in detail in chapter 6.)

Bureaucratic Encounters

Conventional wisdom holds that there is a culture of bureaucracy, that bureaucrats the world over are the same. We
suggest that the way bureaucracy works in each culture is a
reflection of that culture's values. Coping with the bureaucracy in Israel requires a repertoire of skills different from
those required in the United States.

Trying to See the Doctor

A student on a one-year volunteer program in Israel relates
the following incident:

> I was sure that I was coming down with the flu, so I forced
> myself to get out of bed in order to get to the health service.
> I arrived at 8:30, but, by then, all of the numbers had been
> given out. The health clinic is run like a delicatessen; you
> have to take a number and wait. When the nurse saw me
> standing there, she said, "Sorry, the doctor sees only fifteen
> patients, and you got here too late today. No exceptions.
> Take a few aspirin, get into bed, and come back tomorrow."
> I returned to my apartment and did as told. When I described
> what happened to my Israeli neighbor, she said that I had
> given up too quickly, that I could have seen the doctor if I
> had really persisted.

Understanding the American student's behavior is not
very difficult. In American culture, no usually means no.
Rules exist, and there are generally reasons for them. Middle-
class Americans tend to assume that rules are applied fairly,
at least in most cases. The student in the incident had every
reason to believe that the nurse's response was unequivocal.

Accustomed to dealing with myriad bureaucracies, Israelis
operate according to a different set of assumptions. No may
mean no, or it may simply be the first statement in a negotiation. The implicit message may be, "I'm going to say no; now,

let's hear what you're going to say." Or the individual, the nurse in this case, may really intend to transmit no, but she knows that she can be worn down if the patient stubbornly persists.

Israeli patients may use a range of coping strategies (see Appendix A for a fuller discussion of them), but their basic assumption is that the rules can be bent or even broken. Almost everything is negotiable. There is a relatively high tolerance for "testing" behavior. Indeed, in the Israeli mind, testing is frequently synonymous with initiative and the willingness to take risks.

A sick Israeli student may be rewarded for her persistence, i.e., her unwillingness to accept a no, or she may not. She will undoubtedly be ready to make that gamble. The nurse is also expected to show initiative and to use her judgment. The chances of her being reprimanded are slim. Her boss (the doctor) will not scold her for breaking the rules and allowing the student in, even though all the numbers have been given out. She, too, is allowed to bend the rules. No isn't always no as far as her boss is concerned either.

Adapting to the Situation

As in the cases above, ask yourself if you want to change the situation.

If the answer is "no, I feel too lousy," then the most logical behavior is to go home, take two aspirin, and get into bed. Get up earlier the next morning so that you are the first in line to receive a number.

But if the answer is yes, put all your negotiating skills to work. Remember that Israeli bureaucrats can be worn down. They are less likely to stay in role, more willing to reveal their human, social, after-hours, concentric-circles selves. Don't give up when you hear the first no. Be persistent. Test the limits within the parameters of what feels comfortable for you. Example: "I understand that the doctor can only see fifteen patients. Maybe I can just sit here and wait in case one of the patients doesn't show up." (In fact, it's very likely that one of the patients won't show up. People tend to take a number, embark on other errands, and return at the approximate time their number will be called. Sometimes their estimate is correct and sometimes it isn't.) The situation in the doctor's office—the medical bureaucracy—repeats itself in other bureaucratic encounters, e.g., clearing a car at customs or extending a visa at the Interior Ministry. Try to penetrate the rings of concentric circles. You might even want to attempt a little drama. The dying Camille often draws a positive response!

Fear of "Freiing"

No description of Israeli culture would be complete without reference to the term *freier*, which is Hebrew slang for "sucker" or "pushover." Fear of being a freier is embedded in the Israeli character from childhood, and Israelis spend a great deal of energy in the effort not to be one or, at least, not to look like one. If you're an American sojourner, you're likely to hear the word frequently. Indeed, you may be labeled a freier or cautioned about being one.

No one wants to be a sucker, Americans included. In Israel, however, more types of behavior fall under that category than in the U.S. A freier is someone who takes no for an answer, especially from a bureaucrat. A person who always goes according to the rules instead of trying to bend or challenge them is a freier, as is someone who believes that people will do what they say they are going to do. A freier is an individual who falls for a sales pitch, comes out on the wrong side of a deal (for children, being a freier can mean coming out on the short end of a swap), believes what's written in the guarantee, or assumes that the first price offered cannot be negotiated.

Fear of being a freier is only the outer layer of the cultural onion. It rests on a basic assumption: Most people can't be trusted. Given half a chance, they will take advantage of you. It makes sense to distrust others until they give you a reason to trust them; there's less chance of getting hurt. (See discussion of trust as a cultural parameter in chapter 7.) Americans usually don't leave the house in the morning assuming that at some point in the day they are going to act like a sucker or that someone else might play them for a sucker. Many Israelis do. Americans tend to trust others until they are given a reason to distrust them. Most other cultures in the Middle East, Europe, and Asia share the Israelis' fairly jaundiced view of human nature. In other words, Americans tend to be on the far "trust" end of the trust-distrust continuum.

Making sure that you are not a freier, or even more important, making sure you are not perceived as one, is related, we believe, to the casual attitude in Israel toward rules and regulations. If I know that others are likely to disregard the rules, or at least to challenge them and to benefit from doing so, then I'm a freier if I accept them at face value. The American student who tried to see the doctor accepted the nurse's no. Her neighbor told her that she probably could have gotten in despite the nurse's initial refusal. The neighbor didn't tell the student that she was a freier, but that's probably what she thought.

Not being a freier is also related, we believe, to the toughness prized in Israel. Observers, even friends, are more likely to blame the victim for being a freier than they are to blame the person who did the exploiting. If one is a freier, he or she (especially he) has demonstrated weakness, invited exploitation, and shown an inability to take care of him- or herself. Of course, to be or not to be a freier isn't always a life-and-death issue or a metaphysical dilemma. It may simply reflect the slightly jaundiced, cynically humorous manner in which Israelis view themselves and the world. If your friends think you've been a freier, you may be the butt of some good-natured teasing, and everyone, including you, will have a few laughs. Then you'll all forget it. Freier refers to behavior in a particular situation. It's not a lifetime label.

Conclusion

In commercial transactions and bureaucratic encounters between Israelis and Americans, a number of significant cultural differences come into play. As we've seen, they usually center around priorities and preferences. In Israel, in contrast to the U.S., social relationships tend to be at least as important as efficiency. In the U.S., customers tend to be most comfortable with uniform and predictable behavior. In Israel, customers as well as those providing service tend to prefer behavior based on the concentric-circles model of distance-intimacy. Israelis are far less deferential and observe less role distance than do Americans in their commercial and bureaucratic interactions.

Despite the strength of these characteristics among Israelis, even as we write this book, much is changing. The Histadrut network of medical clinics, which most closely resembles an American HMO, has begun the transition to a system where people make appointments instead of competing for early numbers. Israelis are rapidly adopting a Western, American-oriented approach to customer service. This means less time for human contact, an attempt to be more cost effective. You may discover that we've described a worst-case scenario and that many of your commercial encounters will be marked by courteous, efficient service.

Be that as it may, it's still rough out there! One American long-term sojourner commented, "During my stay in Israel, I met the most obnoxious people I have ever encountered as well as the kindest, finest, most helpful ones. The funny thing is that they were often the same people!"

At this point, you might want to take a break and do the coping-strategies exercise in Appendix A. It's enjoyable, especially if you do it in a group, and it should give you an indication of how much concentric-circles penetrating you're willing and able to do.

6

Distance, Deference,
and Dissonance in the Workplace

George, an American manager on a three-year assignment in Israel, describes his relationship with Israeli subordinates:

> My subordinates challenge whatever I ask them to do. In the States, any employee under my authority would understand that I was the boss. Here, everyone is the boss! When I ask a worker to perform a task or carry out an assignment, he counters by saying, "But that doesn't make any sense. We've never done it that way." Or: "We have a better way of dealing with that issue." I find myself getting into arguments and acting very defensively, justifying my actions to my own staff!

Erica, an American academic on sabbatical, describes a similar phenomenon:

> The other day, I witnessed the following scene at the bank: there was a long line, and only two tellers were on duty. Several of the customers complained to Mickey, the bank manager. He, in turn, asked one of the workers in the foreign currency department to move over to the shekel department in order to ease the situation there. Very few customers were waiting in the foreign currency department and twenty people were waiting on line in the shekel withdrawal and deposit

section. The worker, Avi, complained that it wasn't fair, that there was no reason why he should have to stop his work in order to rescue the staff of another department.

When Mickey insisted, Avi got up, walked away, and came back five minutes later. He looked angry, said that he did not like being insulted. Then he sat down and did as Mickey had asked. All of this took place in full view and hearing of me and the other customers. Later, I asked Mickey: "How can you let him talk to you that way?" Mickey said, "It's not so serious. He's a good worker who just has to let off steam. That's the way he is."

Erica was surprised and amused. The incident supplied comic relief during a day of frustrating bureaucratic encounters and it provided her with an excellent anecdote to relate to the family at the dinner table.... "You're not going to believe what happened today at the bank." It is reasonable to assume that her family laughed and moved on to another subject. No doubt they attributed the Israeli employee's behavior to *chutzpah* (gall), the weather (hot!), or childishness. They may have thought that Mickey was a poor manager. And, of course, they agreed that the Mickey-Avi incident would be inconceivable in an American work setting. Few American employees would allow themselves such emotional outbursts and no American manager would tolerate such obvious, public insubordination.

Erica could afford to be amused because she was an observer, a member of the audience in what, for her, resembled a television situation comedy. George, the American manager in the first incident, was not amused. Indeed, he was annoyed and frustrated by what he perceived to be the insubordinate behavior of his staff. The constant friction caused by daily confrontations was wearing him down, and the arguments and explanations seemed counterproductive.

Although one American was amused and the other irritated, both viewed the Israeli behavior as insubordination. As newcomers, however, they had no way of knowing whether the behavior was typical, what it meant in Israeli society, or how it fit into a larger context of common expectations, norms, and behavior patterns.

A closer look at these two incidents brings into focus a key Israeli cultural characteristic: informal patterns of personal interaction. In the workplace, which reflects Israeli society as a whole, informality manifests itself in a singular lack of distance between managers and subordinates and a stubborn tendency to ignore hierarchical roles.

An American consultant on a six-month company assignment in Israel describes her first impression of the workplace:

> When I walked into the office the first day, I saw five staff members sitting around talking. There was no way that I could tell by the way they related to each other, by their outward appearance, by their nonverbal behavior, or by their conversation who was the director or who were senior managers, midlevel managers, first-year engineers, secretaries, or clerks. In the lunchroom, I was confronted by the same scene on a larger scale (there was no executive dining room). I lacked the clues which would help me identify individuals of different status, and I wasn't sure where I was expected to sit or how I was expected to behave.

Historical Roots

Israel's founding fathers and mothers were committed to the creation of a new, egalitarian social order. They rejected the idea of broad differences in income and privilege as well as the ceremonies and trappings of rank. These were viewed as the embodiment of a decadent, exploitative European society. Their egalitarianism expressed itself in an almost exaggerated informality, a deliberate reversal of deferential ways of speaking and behaving. In certain respects, the Israeli founding generation can be compared to the early Protestant settlers who came to the American colonies. Their white, Anglo-Saxon behavior patterns and norms became the model for successive waves of newcomers; indeed, the model was often imposed on unwilling immigrants. For long years (many would argue, to this very day), assimilation into the American mainstream was synonymous with the adoption of early Puritan or Anglo-Saxon behavior patterns. A similar process has occurred in Israel, where the beliefs and norms of the founding generation continue to have a profound impact on current-day behavior.

Lack of distance, egalitarianism, inattention to hierarchy, informality are all terms used to describe American as well as Israeli society. Yet as informal and nonhierarchical as Americans are, Israelis are more so. Americans who understand that will be better able to make sense out of what they experience in the Israeli workplace. The real challenge, however, is to understand the connection between Israeli informality and other norms, expectations, and behavior patterns they encounter there. We'll explore that connection in the following incidents.

An Informal Discussion

This incident is related by Tom Richards, a consultant on quality assurance for the U.S. Department of Defense.

> My employer, the Defense Department, had been working with an Israeli firm for two years. The firm had undertaken to design and produce one of the components of a sophisticated communications system. The incident took place during the stage when the Israelis were producing the prototype and testing its subcomponents.
>
> I was asked to accompany Mike Carpenter to Israel. Mike was the technical director of the project for the Defense Department. He had met the Israeli team several times and they had established a good working relationship. Besides, they were in almost daily contact by phone or fax. I hadn't met anyone on the Israeli team, nor had I ever been with Israelis or visited their country.

Mike took advantage of the long flight to fill me in. "These guys are excellent engineers. They're creative and know how to solve problems. And they're easy to get along with, informal like us. You'll be impressed. Don't worry. I don't understand Hebrew either. Their English is good and they'll explain everything you want to know."

On the first day of our three-day visit, we accompanied Yossi, the technical director, on a tour of the production line. I was impressed by Yossi's knowledge, his command of English, and his affability. By the end of the tour, we had been brought up to date. We were also aware of the problems that had arisen during this stage of the project.

After the tour, we sat down in Yossi's office for an informal meeting. The participants included Yossi, five engineers on his staff, Mike, and me. The most important item in the discussion had to do with a particular test. The test was problematic, because it was supposed to take an entire week. Yossi reported, however, that he and his team had just come up with an idea on how to run the test in a shorter time without changing the "tolerance" that had been written into the original specifications.

Yossi began to explain the team's proposal. About five minutes into his presentation, everything started to fall apart. Three of the staff members started to speak among themselves in Hebrew. Then they interrupted him. Yossi said something, obviously an attempt to keep them quiet. The same thing happened again. He then turned to us and said:

"I hope that you won't mind if we speak in Hebrew for a minute or two. It concerns a solution to the testing problem." Mike: "Sure, no problem. Do you want us to leave?" Yossi: "There's no need."

We sat and witnessed the "performance" for five more minutes. I felt uncomfortable. In fact, I was annoyed with Mike. He should have insisted that we leave. Although I didn't understand a word of the Hebrew, I had the feeling that they were having a major argument. The group was very animated and things seemed tense. Their voices became louder, though they weren't shouting. They seemed to be under pressure. And I realized that they had no respect for

Yossi as a boss. In fact, if I hadn't been told he was the boss, I'd have had no way of knowing that, by their behavior or his.

After five minutes, Yossi resumed the meeting. He apologized for the delay, but explained that the team had arrived at an even better solution than the one he had started to present before the interruption. We listened to the new plan, asked several questions and finally decided to accept it.

In the short run, I was pleased. Mike was right. The Israelis are talented. They come up with original solutions to problems, even though a lot of their ideas seem to come at the last minute. I'm concerned, however, about the long-run implications of what I witnessed. They seem to waste a lot of time. Things are out of control. They have a hard time meeting deadlines and staying within the guidelines. Besides, if the project manager spends so much time dealing with discipline problems, arguments, and challenges to his authority, the project will be delayed.

Despite the discussion with Mike on the plane, Tom was surprised by the way in which the staff related to Yossi, their communication style, and the public nature of the professional discussion. Perhaps Mike hadn't warned him sufficiently. It is possible that he had grown accustomed to the staff's work style and no longer noticed those elements which Tom found troublesome. What matters is that Tom came away from the encounter with serious concerns about the professional behavior of Yossi and his staff and their ability to stay on schedule.

Tom, of course, describes the incident from an American cultural perspective, i.e., a set of expectations and norms concerning privacy, communication style in a professional setting, and the manner in which workers relate to managers.

Yossi and his staff came to the meeting with a different set of expectations and norms. The cultural differences explain some of the misunderstandings on both sides.

Challenging and questioning superiors is inherent in the Israeli work style. Although each manager has his or her personal way of dealing with subordinates, few Israeli managers make a point of maintaining social and professional distance. In practical terms, this means that they encourage subordinates to challenge ideas, suggest modifications, and come up with new and better ways of approaching a problem. For the most part, subordinates feel free to question and confront. They need not be anxious about their jobs nor afraid of being reprimanded, demoted, or otherwise threatened for not deferring to their boss's superior position in the administrative hierarchy. Indeed, those who fail to question assumptions or suggest ideas of their own are often perceived as lacking initiative.[1]

It can be argued, of course, that American managers also expect initiative from their subordinates and are pleased when employees offer counterproposals or pose questions about the feasibility of certain solutions. Questioning superiors, however, was not the only issue in "An Informal Discussion."

Tom's response had to do with the *style* in which Yossi's staff challenged the decision and the *improvisational manner* in which they arrived at a solution at least as much as it had to do with the content of their argument. Indeed, Tom had no way of knowing the content, since he didn't understand Hebrew. What he did pick up was the animation, the voice tones, the confrontation, and the excitement.

---

[1] See Geert Hofstede, *Culture's Consequences: International Differences in Work-Related Values*. Beverly Hills: Sage, 1980. Hofstede examines the effect of cultural differences in the workplace, particularly as they concern attitudes. One of the dimensions along which value systems vary is power distance—equality or inequality in superior-subordinate relations. Israel placed second to the bottom (Austria was last) among forty cultures in power distance. In other words, relative to the other countries in the study, Israel is characterized by a marked degree of equality in superior-subordinate relations.

Israelis are not uncomfortable with direct confrontation in a professional setting, nor do they view it as aggressive. The Israeli communication style is direct, spontaneous, and quite often confrontational. If people are excited or enthusiastic about an idea, they have few inhibitions about showing it. And if an individual presents a weak argument or a proposal which doesn't seem to make sense, he or she can expect an unqualified negative response from colleagues.

One is less likely to hear "It seems to me…," "I suggest…," "Perhaps we should…" in an Israeli conversation than in a parallel conversation among professional colleagues in the U.S. This is especially true among members of a work team irrespective of differences in rank. Israelis will say "You're wrong," "It won't work," "Why didn't you think about…."

Because relatively small value is placed on holding back, at least as it applies to expressions of anger or dissatisfaction, Israelis do not have to be excessively concerned about maintaining a professional tone of voice in the workplace. Shouting, screaming, or having a temper tantrum are considered inappropriate, but raising one's voice in the heat of a discussion or gesturing dramatically with one's hands are acceptable. Tom was put off by the nonverbal aspects of the Israeli communication style. He was convinced that the staff was engaged in a heated argument when, in fact, they were merely having a lively, uninhibited discussion about a point of concern to the entire team.

American professionals, of course, are not always under control. They, too, put a premium on speaking directly. Here the difference between the two cultures expresses itself in the degree to which spontaneity and directness are tolerated, the settings to which they are confined, and the range of sanctions employed to punish those whose behavior is perceived as inappropriate.

The improvisational work style of the Israelis was also at issue here and, to a large extent, it revealed the imprint of their army experience. Yossi's staff was accustomed to coming up with improvised solutions to problems. Indeed, they equated improvisation with creativity. In the incident that Tom narrates, the staff did, in fact, demonstrate an ability to think quickly, bounce ideas around, and come up with a better idea on the spot even if it meant throwing out blueprints, changing programming, and surprising their boss and the American visitors. All of these surprises contributed to Tom's discomfort.

Two very different attitudes toward privacy figure prominently in the incident. Tom was upset because the discussion took place while he and Mike were present. He was uncomfortable and embarrassed, because he expected that an intense discussion about an internal matter would take place in private or at least not in the presence of clients. Mike knew this and hinted to Yossi: "Do you want us to leave?" Yossi didn't pick up the hint because, for him, privacy wasn't a significant issue.

From an American perspective, it seems that every matter in Israel is discussed in public. While this is certainly not the case, it is true that Israelis are comfortable conducting an argument or questioning an idea in a public forum, even if the argument is with their boss and his or her idea is the one that is being torn apart. Naturally, the issue of personal style also comes into play. Each Israeli manager determines the extent to which a confrontation will be tolerated, from whom, and how often. And, of course, every corporation has its own organizational culture.

Implicit in the incident are two definitions of professionalism. Yossi and his team had a perception of professionalism in keeping with the overall Israeli definition: professionalism means having good background knowledge and well-developed skills as well as the ability and the desire to utilize them to achieve defined goals. A real pro in Israeli terms is a "doer" who is committed to the project and the team.

Tom, however, thought that the Israeli behavior was inappropriate and unprofessional. His impressions stemmed from the style in which the discussion was carried on rather than its content or results. The American definition of professionalism is more comprehensive than the Israeli one. It includes not only technical knowledge and the ability to implement it but also demeanor, communication style, and the manner in which one interacts with colleagues. In American terms, unprofessional behavior includes washing one's dirty linen in public, speaking in a loud tone of voice, demonstrating disrespect for one's boss, and wasting colleagues' or clients' time. According to these criteria, the Israelis at the meeting acted in a decidedly unprofessional manner.

Yossi and his staff would undoubtedly have been surprised by Tom's reaction and the inferences he drew. The staff had enormous respect for Yossi. There were no authority problems. They were involved in the project and worked long hours. The team got along well and enjoyed the directness and forcefulness of their professional discussions. They probably regretted speaking Hebrew in the presence of the Americans. That was rude, but it enabled them to communicate with each other more rapidly and accurately.

Yossi took a calculated risk. He knew that the Americans or at least Tom, the newcomer, might get the impression the staff was undisciplined. But neither did he want them to think the Israelis were holding back, keeping secrets. He was sure the Americans would feel excluded if he asked them to leave the room. Yossi apologized for the interruption. In this case, however, the final result justified the staff's behavior. They came up with an excellent solution to the problem. Yossi was proud of their professionalism as he and his staff understood the term.

In "An Informal Discussion," cultural differences connected with work style, communication style, privacy, and the relationship or distance between managers and subordinates were the dominant issues. These same issues, and some additional ones, come into play in more formal settings.

First Impressions

The narrator is John Kirkland, a senior manager for an American electronics firm.

Our company was in the final stages of negotiating the purchase of a sophisticated communications system from an Israeli contractor. I was in charge of coordinating all aspects of the project, whose estimated duration was two years. The Israeli company had agreed to assign one of their staff, Amnon Harel, to our headquarters in the U.S. Amnon was a product-line expert. He was to serve as liaison—troubleshooter—between our staff and theirs. We had been told that he had had considerable experience in the field and was accustomed to coordinating projects of this nature.

The incident occurred a few days after Amnon arrived in the U.S. He attended the first in a series of meetings that was scheduled over the course of a week. The twenty participants included representatives from several departments in our company. The purpose of the series of meetings was to begin coordinating all aspects of this complex undertaking and to iron out major problems. I served as chair. He was the only Israeli present, the sole representative of the contractor.

After the preliminaries—an introduction and overview of the program for the week—we moved to the first item on the morning's agenda, a discussion of the timetable. John Dinnerman, the technical director, presented a detailed plan for replacing our existing system with the new Israeli one. His presentation lasted twenty minutes and it included charts, graphs, and computer printouts. When he finished, I asked for responses from the participants. I didn't single out anyone in particular.

Almost before the question "Would anyone care to respond?" was out of my mouth, Amnon raised his hand and immediately started speaking:

"I want to talk about parts 3 and 4 of the plan. They're impractical because you haven't taken into account the Israeli production process and the need for reevaluation and communication across the Atlantic. I've had a lot of experience on projects of this nature and I've been working on this project since it was initiated in Israel, so I know that it will be impossible to meet the dates on the timetable."

I could sense the tension in the room. The man was acting as if he had known us for months and was having a casual argument about the relative merits of two football teams! In fact, it was the first time most of the Americans had met him. I could hear alarm bells ringing in my head. I suggested that we suspend further discussion of the subject and move on to the next item on the agenda.

Amnon failed to conform to the chair's and other participants' expectations about appropriate behavior at a formal meeting, especially the first one in a series. Equally important, perhaps, was his failure to conform to American role expectations. The Israeli was a newcomer, he hadn't met the participants before, he was a representative of the contractor, and he was attending a meeting in the client's territory. In the eyes of the Americans, these roles conferred upon him a lower status than the other participants in the meeting. His behavior was expected to be in accordance with his status.

It is reasonable to assume that the chair expected the Israeli representative to either say nothing at the first meeting or to wait until he had been addressed. If Amnon did volunteer to speak, he was expected to wait until participants with a higher status had spoken.

A society which cares about formality and hierarchy provides answers to the following questions: What is my role in this situation? How am I supposed to act in this role? In the Israeli workplace, as in Israeli society as a whole, these issues have little relevance. Instead, a different set of questions is asked: "What is my goal and how can I best reach it?" (The preference for goals over roles also explains the Israeli tendency to bypass authority, even in situations where the Israeli is the contractor and the American is the client. Impatient with what they perceive as decision-making dithering by middle managers, Israeli contractors will often jump several levels and take their problems to company vice presidents.)

The difficulty experienced by the Israeli in conforming to the chair's expectations stemmed, in part, from his lack of exposure to situations in which hierarchical relationships are clearly defined, professional behavior is a function of role, and the transition from formal to informal behavior occurs more slowly.

In the Israeli work environment, of course, individuals do distinguish between the roles of client and vendor, and Israeli behavior at a first meeting with strangers is more reserved than it would be at a meeting where they know all the participants. However, behavior which is a function of role (newcomer, foreigner, sole representative of the contractor), is less clearly defined. Distance and deference are maintained for shorter periods. After a relatively short time (as little as half an hour), hierarchical and status relationships, loosely defined to begin with, become blurred and interactions become more informal. Participants discover that they know people in common, were in the same army unit, or attended the university together. All these events occur at a rapid pace.

Cultural differences around the issue of pace were underlined in the incident by different perceptions of time and timing. How does one measure "waiting for someone to speak" or "waiting one's turn?" According to the American account of the incident, the Israeli response was immediate. Amnon didn't wait to see if anyone else wanted to speak. Instead, he plunged right in with his own views. It's entirely conceivable, however, that Amnon assumed that he had waited long enough to allow others to volunteer. Israeli "air space," i.e., the interval of time between individual A's last word and individual B's first word, tends to be shorter than American air space; indeed, A and B's words frequently overlap.

The timing of Amnon's response is also related to the issue of self-confidence. It is impossible to discuss self-confidence without referring, once again, to the cultural imprint of Israel's founding fathers and mothers. They not only wanted to create an egalitarian society, the antithesis of the Eastern European society they had rejected, they also wanted to create a new Jew who would be the antithesis of the Jew in the Diaspora. They perceived the Diaspora Jew as fearful, needlessly deferential, and overly conscious of authority. The new Jew was to be fearless and self-confident; and he or she would use every opportunity to prove it.

To this day, Israeli behavior patterns bear the mark of this early cultural dynamic. Demonstrations of self-confidence are highly valued. In professional settings, self-confidence expresses itself in the willingness to state one's views not only forcefully, but immediately. In many situations, silence is viewed as a lack of self-confidence.

Self-confidence is valued as a positive trait in American society as well. Why, then, is Israeli self-confidence so grating? Why do Americans, almost universally, view Israeli self-confidence as arrogance? Part of the answer, it seems, lies in the different ways in which self-confidence is expressed.

Americans are taught to combine self-confidence with displays of modesty. The strong, silent type who doesn't have to prove anything is a familiar character in American movies and books. Israelis, on the other hand, seem to be under pressure to prove that they are not afraid, that they know what they are talking about. In the American mind, if you are really self-confident, it is unnecessary to prove yourself all the time.

Different ways of displaying self-confidence are a source of major cultural misunderstandings between Americans and Israelis, especially in business settings. Americans tend to perceive Israelis as arrogant know-it-alls. Israelis tend to mistake American silence and sense of timing, the feeling that they don't have to hurry to prove what they know, as lack of confidence. Sometimes they even conclude that Americans have no backbone.

Analysis of the incident also reveals significant differences in communication style. If the Israeli representative had simply spoken out of turn or failed to address the chair with the proper deference ("I have a few remarks to make, if I may"), the American manager might have attributed his behavior to a lack of experience at formal meetings. It is clear, however, that the chair reacted to the *manner* in which the Israeli representative transmitted his remarks.

Amnon failed to speak in the proper code for a business meeting. He neither acknowledged the twenty-minute opening presentation nor offered a few positive remarks. (Americans tend to preface criticism with praise or appreciation in order to communicate the fact that the criticism does not emanate from dislike of the person being criticized nor from a negative judgment of the person as a human being.) Instead, Amnon criticized the plan in direct, unequivocal terms. "They're impractical...," "I know that it will be impossible...." He appeared to make no effort to soften his remarks or to present them in a tentative manner by using such expressions as "It seems to me...," "You might want to take a look at...," "Have you thought about...." Amnon's extraordinary directness combined with his repeated use of "I" ("I've had a lot of experience"), contributed to the impression that he was rude, aggressive, and egocentric. (See the discussion of dugri speech in chapter 4.)

Many Israeli professionals would find Amnon's behavior acceptable, especially if the content of his remarks made sense. Israelis tend to be extraordinarily practical as well as thick-skinned. Style matters less than content.

Despite differences between the Israeli and American communication styles, it would be a mistake to conclude that Amnon's behavior would always be acceptable in Israel. He might very well be viewed as arrogant, especially if his only goal was to talk about himself. The cultural differences revolve around the severity of the response, that is, the personal and organizational sanctions that are likely to be imposed. If Israelis disapproved of Amnon's behavior, they might challenge him in an equally confrontational style. There might be friction in the room, but it would not make the other participants feel uncomfortable. Indeed, it would be viewed, as it was in "An Informal Discussion," as an integral part of the work process.

The chairman of an open discussion in Israel might reprimand Amnon directly in the presence of the other participants. "You're way out of line." Then the incident would be forgotten. It is possible, but extremely unlikely, that Amnon's behavior in Israel, among Israelis, would damage his career advancement. Nor would such directness be likely to affect the overall estimate of his professional abilities.

Amnon's behavior was out of line, in part because he failed to stay within the confines of his role as the representative of the contractor. From an American perspective, the key issue is one of boundaries, the Israeli inability or unwillingness to stay within the borders of the picture in the metaphorical coloring book. Here are some additional examples:

1. On his first day of work in the American parent company, an Israeli engineer noticed that there were four clocks on the wall in the reception area. The clocks displayed the time in each of the company's four subsidiaries, one of which was located in Israel. The engineer noticed that the time on the clock for the Israeli subsidiary had not been corrected for daylight savings time. He calmly climbed on a chair (not a ladder!), removed the face from the clock, adjusted the time, climbed down, and returned the chair to its place. His American colleagues looked on in amazement.

2. Two teams, American and Israeli, were working jointly to develop a software product. Most of the work was taking place in the United States, although the Israeli team was split between the United States and Israel. Both teams were under pressure to meet a deadline.

The manager of the Israeli team approached one of the software people on the American team.

Israeli: "We have to have this completed by the end of the day. I need you to drop everything and build the software release."

American: "I'll have to confirm my priorities with my boss."

Israeli: "Your boss isn't available. I'm asking you to do it."

American: "I'll do it as soon as humanly possible."

Israeli: "If you can't do it, I'll take care of it myself."

The American worker complained afterwards that the Israeli was pushy, aggressive, and demanding:

"Instead of explaining why completion of the work was urgent and then allowing me or my boss to make a judgment about priorities, he intruded into our professional territory and tried to take over ownership of the task."

3. An Israeli software team was working at the American parent company. The company was shut down during the week between Christmas and New Year's so that its employees could enjoy a vacation. The Israeli team chose not to take the vacation days. Instead they planned to use the time to complete several urgent tasks. When they arrived at the office, the Israelis discovered that the management had contracted with an outside company to carry out "preventive maintenance." The entire computer system was to be shut down for twenty-four hours. Determined to complete the task the team had assigned itself, the Israeli manager called Operations and took it upon himself to cancel the preventive maintenance order even though it meant that mangagement would have to find another time to shut down the system. The Israelis proceeded with their work. When his superior returned from vacation, the Israeli manager informed him that he had signed the order canceling the preventive main-

tenance so that his team could meet the deadline. He also informed his boss that their efforts had paid off. They met their deadline and the product was ready for delivery to the customer.

We conducted an informal test of American and Israeli reactions to the anecdote about the wall clocks. Americans laughed; they found the Israeli behavior startling. Most Americans reported that it would never occur to them to adjust the clock. They would either say nothing or politely inform the person in charge who would then call on the maintenance department to make the adjustment. Several Israeli respondents indicated that they would act as the Israeli employee had. Others said that they might not do anything at all. But the Israelis had a hard time understanding why the Americans found the Israeli behavior so strange.

In another informal survey, we asked both Americans and Israelis to provide a word to describe the Israeli behavior in the last two examples. Although there was some overlap, i.e, instances in which Israelis and Americans used the same words to describe the Israeli behavior, Israeli responses clustered around the words "initiative," "creative," "active," "improvisational," "persistent." American responses clustered around the following words: "intrusive," "aggressive," "out of line," "invasive," "insubordinate," "pushy." Interestingly, all of the above words relate to the issue of border crossings. In the case of the last example—canceling the preventive maintenance order—the word "inconsiderate" was added. The issue went beyond the Israeli manager's exceeding the limits of his authority. By solving the problem according to its priorities, the small Israeli team *created* a problem for the large group of Americans returning from vacation. (We're reminded of the parking lot illustration in chapter 4.) Preventive maintenance, involving the shutting down of the computer system, would now have to be carried out when the majority of employees were back at work. Those employees would have difficulties meeting *their* deadlines.

Our discussion of American-Israeli cultural differences in the workplace raises an important question: Once Israelis understand that certain aspects of their behavior may be inappropriate in an American environment, how easy is it for them to adapt to a different set of norms and expectations? Do they choose to do so at all? The answer, as always, begins with the words "It depends." It depends primarily on what one has to give up and what one gains.

Israeli professionals exposed to American work norms for a considerable period of time usually make a serious attempt, for example, to soften sandpapery dugri speech. They do so even though they continue to believe that speaking dugri is a more honest form of communication than indirect speech.

Once they learn that Israeli give-and-take between managers and subordinates may be perceived by Americans as insubordination and/or lack of discipline, Israeli managers insist on holding those discussions when Americans are not present. They also develop strategies for damage control if and when their subordinates forget the norms and fail to conform to American expectations.

In short, experienced Israeli professionals are unlikely to act like Amnon in "First Impressions" or the Israeli project manager in "An Informal Discussion." In these instances, the smoother working relationships that one gains with American colleagues and clients outweigh the costs. Softening dugri speech requires an effort, but one doesn't have to sacrifice the message behind the words; working teams may have to restrain themselves in the presence of outsiders, but they can resume their give-and-take relationship with their boss as soon as the outsiders leave.

When it comes to border crossings of the kind discussed in the second and third examples, however, the balance between pain and gain often reverses itself. Israeli professionals are not always sensitive to the nuances of boundaries, but they know that pushing a point, failing to go through channels, or intruding into someone else's professional territory exacts a price. It may be a raised eyebrow, or the heavier price of strained work relationships and reinforcement of a negative stereotype of Israelis. On the other hand, experience has taught them that when they cross boundaries, things get done.

Israelis are loath to compromise the very qualities that they believe give them the competitive edge over their counterparts in other countries. As defined by Israelis, those qualities include the willingness to accept responsibility, assume initiative, and change what needs to be changed even if rules are broken, feelings are hurt, and someone is inconvenienced. Americans look at the behavior in which Israelis see these qualities expressed and give it a different label: insubordination and intrusiveness. (See "Same Behavior/Separate Labels: The Differences at a Glance" for a detailed comparison of Israeli/American perceptions of themselves and each other.)

Clearly, there are situations in which Israelis will decide that conformity to American border-crossing norms is advisable. When Israelis are careful not to exceed the boundaries of their job descriptions or other people's perceptions of where their authority ends and someone else's begins, they pay a heavy internal price. Their behavior is in direct contradiction to a lifetime of social and mental programming.

Many of us remember the "dare" scenario from elementary school: "I dare you to...." "Oh yeah?" "Yeah!" Accepting the dare proved that you had the "right stuff." Israeli adults, particularly men, seem to have internalized the dare scenario and adapted it to the demands of adolescence and adulthood. Before, during, and after army service, individuals who take charge, change what has to be changed instead of waiting for or following instructions, figure out innovative ways of accomplishing a task, and take the risk of doing all of these things when the odds do not seem to be in their favor are rewarded with approval and the more tangible prize of promotion to leadership positions. In the Israeli view, they are ideal candidates to become team leaders or project managers. Indeed, "He's a pusher" or "He's a bulldozer" are often used as expressions of approval. ("*She's* a bulldozer" can be used pejoratively, however.)

A senior Israeli manager responsible for selecting service engineers for assignment in the U.S. explained his dilemma: "I hire engineers because they have initiative, assume responsibility, and get things done. Then, before I send them on assignment to the U.S., I have to tell them to "put a lid on it," to be very careful about displaying Israeli initiative in an American work environment. I warn them that they may be perceived as arrogant, pushy, and out of line. In short, I'm asking them to erase twenty or thirty years of social conditioning and professional training. And by constraining them, I also run the risk of making them less effective."

American managers also hire people who display initiative and an ability to get things done. Americans are darers and risk takers as well, yet their risk taking differs from that of Israelis. Israelis look at American risk taking and see caution. Americans look at Israeli risk taking and see irresponsibility and foolhardiness. Perhaps the difference lies in the respective attitudes toward boundaries. In this case, boundaries represent the edge. Americans seem willing to risk up to the edge, and they build in backup systems or contingency plans. Israelis go over the edge. They often hold their breath and take a flying leap with complete self-confidence that they will land safely or will be able to "handle it."

An example of different attitudes toward risk taking can be seen in entrepreneurial approaches to new business ventures. Both Israeli and American entrepreneurs are willing to embark on new business ventures in areas that haven't yet been explored. They move into the unknown with the knowledge that there are no guarantees and that the venture may fail. Americans, however, are much better prepared when they embark on a new venture. They have a business plan which they intend to follow. They have worked out the probabilities of success and failure and approach the venture as a chess game. The initial moves have been carefully plotted in advance, and, in many cases, plan B is available if plan A fails. Israelis have a business plan, because the bank and other authorities require it, not necessarily because they intend to follow it. The business plan is based on less systematic research than the American plan, and it contains fewer backup systems or contingency plans. There seems to be the implicit belief that things will work out.

Adapting to the Situation

Thus far, our analysis has focused on American-Israeli cultural differences in the workplace as well as the issue of Israeli adaptation to American norms and expectations. How, in contrast, do Americans adapt to Israeli norms?

That adaptation involves three principal variables: role relationships (these include client-contractor, manager-subordinate, and colleague-colleague); the location in which the interaction takes place (U.S. or Israel), and the cultural identity of the individual in each role (American or Israeli).

Presented graphically, American-Israeli interactions in the workplace occur in the following contexts:

Role Relationships

American client/Israeli contractor in the U.S./Israel
American contractor/Israeli client in the U.S./Israel
American manager/Israeli subordinate in the U.S./Israel
American subordinate/Israeli manager in the U.S./Israel
American colleague/Israeli colleague in the U.S./Israel
American colleague/Israeli colleague, one in U.S./ one in Israel

If one is an American client dealing with an Israeli contractor, one often has the luxury of calling the shots: compelling the contractor to conform to American norms. Israeli contractors or suppliers know that the client has the option of reprimanding the contractor, insisting on certain behavior, canceling the contract, and/or refusing to do business with that firm in the future. However, Israeli contractors are not always convinced that "the customer is always right" and are not bashful about saying so. If the American in this relationship is the *contractor* dealing with an Israeli *client*, the Israeli has the luxury of calling the shots. American contractors would be more reluctant about contradicting their Israeli customers. In most cases, the geographical setting in which the client-contractor interaction takes place has little impact on behavior.

American managers dealing with Israeli subordinates in the U.S. have the luxury of knowing that their subordinates are under pressure to adapt to American work norms. If the American manager is supervising employees in Israel, the balance begins to shift. Managerial behavior which goes against the grain, i.e., causes dissonance, may result in open resistance or, at the very least, strained work relationships. After all, the American is the stranger even if he or she is the boss.

The balance shifts to an even greater degree if the American is the subordinate and the Israeli is the manager or supervisor in Israel. Then, of course, the American is under considerable pressure to adapt to Israeli expectations, norms, and behavior patterns.

If the American is the subordinate and the Israeli is the manager or supervisor in the U.S., there is pressure on the Israeli to adapt to American norms; simultaneously, being in a position of authority, the Israeli can impose his or her own expectations on subordinates. The clash of different sets of expectations creates dissonance in the organization and massive confusion among the individuals involved.

There are many situations in which Americans and Israelis working on joint projects act as trans-Atlantic colleagues, i.e, they are in constant written and spoken communication, but rarely, if ever, visit each other's turf. If they are to function as a multicultural team or, at the very least, communicate effectively in the absence of face-to-face interactions, both groups are compelled to demonstrate mutual flexibility about adapting to each other's norms. Americans, for example, have to make an effort to adopt a more direct written and spoken communication style, and Israelis have to tone down their sandpapery speech.

In collegial relationships involving visits to the other's turf, however, the visitor is expected to exhibit greater flexibility. Israelis in Israel feel less compelled to alter their communication style. American visitors participating in technical discussions with colleagues in Israel usually have to accustom themselves to a higher level of verbal confrontation. Another, more obvious example concerns the pressure to dress according to local norms. American professionals accustomed to coming to work in a suit and, for men, a tie, expect visiting Israeli colleagues to dress in a similar fashion. When those same American professionals come to Israel, they are expected to replace their suits and ties with the more informal Israeli attire of open-necked shirt and sports slacks or blouse and skirt/pants.

We have deliberately formulated the above distinctions primarily in terms of the American mindset: pressure to adapt as a function of role. Indeed, for an American, acting according to one's role seems natural and right. If we examine the same distinctions in terms of the Israeli mindset, they make less sense. The American tendency to view behavior as a function of *role* vis-à-vis the Israeli tendency to view behavior as a function of *goals* was discussed in detail above. In the critical incident "First Impressions," for example, the perception that the Israeli behavior toward the client was out of role in American terms caused considerable friction. Amnon was a representative of the contractor at a formal meeting, but he didn't meet the American expectations concerning the deference and distance required of someone in his role.

Given the roles versus goals dichotomy as well as the cultural differences discussed in this chapter, it is useful to return to the set of questions formulated in chapter 3:

1. Do I care enough to change the situation?

2. If so:

    a. Can I change the environment which is causing me discomfort or anxiety without altering my behavior, i.e., without adapting to Israeli norms, expectations, and behavior patterns? If not, and I must adapt:

    b. In what *situations* am I willing and able to adapt?

    c. To what *extent* am I willing and able to adapt?

Practical Implications

Following are suggested strategies for getting along with Israelis in a work environment. The strategies are organized according to the cultural issues analyzed in this chapter. They are meant to broaden your repertoire of coping-strategies and are based on the assumption that the goal of adaptation in the workplace is to maximize productivity, increase efficiency, and avoid unnecessary communication breakdowns.

Communication Style, Self-Confidence, and Pace

Adopt a direct communication style. Do so at an earlier juncture than you would if you were dealing with Americans. Bear in mind that the pace of moving from stranger to "one of the gang" is much faster than it is in the U.S. workplace. Remember, Israelis tend to be on "fast-forward." They prefer a direct style with an unequivocal message to one in which the message is open to interpretation. Drop or minimize softeners like "It seems to me," "Perhaps I'm wrong but...," and "Don't you think that...," which give the impression that you are wishy-washy and lack self-confidence.

(Of course, at the same time that you are reading this, Israeli professionals are participating in workshops in which they are studying how to communicate with Americans and practicing a less direct, less confrontational style of communication! They are learning to *insert* expressions like "It seems to me...," "Perhaps we should...," "Have you thought about...?" and are working on exercises in which they sensitize themselves to the American mindset.)

A word of caution: Beware of the "Attila the Hun" syndrome. Every confrontation doesn't have to be an explosion. In your attempts to be "more Israeli than the Israelis," you may overdo your efforts at adaptation. You may be more direct, assertive, and confrontational than the occasion demands. Israelis may turn to each other and say: "Who is this arrogant American?"

Manager-Subordinate Relationships

If you are managing Israeli subordinates, try to view their questioning of your directives in the context of the Israeli work style. Keep in mind that the distance between managers and subordinates is much narrower than it is in the U.S., that goals are usually more important than roles, that arguments and questioning are often a useful way to solve problems creatively, that managers tend to view themselves as members of a work team. Show a willingness to question their suggestions as much as they question yours.

You may discover that your readiness to hold your own in a free-for-all discussion with your subordinates increases productivity and efficiency and enhances the impression that you know how to do your job. Your demonstration of knowledge and expertise, as well as the respect you show for the knowledge and expertise of your subordinates, will strengthen your status. You will diminish your status if you pull rank and hide behind an administrative title.

Decide for yourself, however, whether you are willing to move further along the adaptation scale to the point, for example, where you accept arguments and questioning by your staff in the presence of outsiders.

Whose Job Is It Anyway?
Goals versus Roles Priorities

If you are managing an Israeli staff or working with Israeli colleagues, assume that border crossing will be the rule rather than the exception. Expect your subordinates or colleagues to exceed the boundaries of their job descriptions, to try to determine other people's priorities, and to make decisions without consulting the appropriate individuals, including you.

Do not assume that Israeli colleagues or subordinates will be able to discern all of the boundaries that Americans take for granted. Define boundaries carefully. Set limits. Assume that the limits will be tested. Then, choose your battles; in other words, weigh the trade-offs. You may decide that having an Israeli colleague determine your priorities for you is counterproductive; indeed, you may find the behavior intolerable. Say so. There may be situations in which your insistence that Israeli subordinates obtain permission before they proceed with each step of a marketing plan increases efficiency. In other instances, your "stop, look, and listen" approach may dampen enthusiasm, diminish creativity, and foster resistance.

If you are the subordinate of an Israeli manager, experiment with Israeli "take charge" behavior. Don't ask. Decide what you think should be done. Do it. Inform your boss about what you are doing and let him or her know that you are willing to risk a reprimand (or worse) if things don't work out as you plan.

Collegial Relationships

Research suggests that the multicultural teams which are most effective are those which pay attention to process—*how* things are done. Multicultural teams which ignore or minimize the *how* and focus primarily on the *what*—bottom-line results—are often ineffective. Communication breakdowns, stress, and mistrust inhibit their productivity.[2]

If you are working with Israeli colleagues, take the time to anticipate the differences likely to affect behavior and to find out what makes them feel comfortable on a team. Explain how you are used to doing things, and negotiate goals and procedures everyone can live with. You'll expend considerable energy, but it won't be wasted.

Work versus Social Life/Public versus Private Persona

Schedule time for social interactions in the workplace. Your colleagues and subordinates will feel more comfortable; the impression that you care may very well increase productivity and motivation.

If you are working in Israel either as a colleague or manager, make a point of attending your coworkers' family celebrations, e.g., weddings and bar mitzvahs. Failure to do so will be viewed with greater severity than it would be in the U.S., where there is a clearer line drawn between work and social life.

If you are willing to move further along the scale, you might want to consider giving your subordinates leeway to attend their children's holiday celebrations at school or bring children into work during school vacations. In the short run,

---

[2] Nancy Adler, *International Dimensions of Organizational Behavior*. Boston: Kent, 1986, 106.

productivity will probably decrease; in the long run, it may well rise because subordinates will be more willing to come in after work hours to finish important projects.

If you are an American client or colleague engaged in an ongoing professional relationship with an Israeli colleague, invite that person to your home when he or she is in the U.S. for business. Israelis will be gratified by your invitation and your willingness to blur the line between work and social life. Most Israelis are under the impression that Americans never invite people to their homes, that they spend their time entertaining in a relatively formal restaurant setting. This misunderstanding, we believe, stems from cultural differences in the pace and ceremony surrounding hospitality.

Americans, of course, do invite American colleagues to their homes, but the invitation will occur at a relatively later stage in the professional relationship, and it will usually signal a willingness to make a deeper commitment. Indeed, the invitation to one's home may be preceded by a sequence of other social interactions, each of which reveals a different level of commitment: lunch during the workday, drinks after work, dinner at a restaurant. Because they usually skip the intermediate stages and invite friends and colleagues to their homes at a much earlier point, Israelis are sometimes hurt by what they perceive as distance and coldness in American hospitality.

(Before going on to the next chapter, we suggest that you do the coping-strategies exercise in Appendix B.)

7

Have We Made a Deal Yet?
Israeli Negotiating Style

Virtually all of the issues discussed in the last chapter, as well as several others, come into play in the negotiation process. They may be no more than irritants—cross-cultural static. On the other hand, they may prove to be the source of serious misunderstandings or unintended insults. They might even cause the negotiations to break down.

If you are going to negotiate an agreement with Israelis, it's probably a good idea to develop reasonable expectations about the Israeli negotiating style. There are wide variations in that style, since it is a function of several factors. These include:

- the personalities of the individuals involved

- the particular Israeli corporate culture of which they are a part

- exposure and degree of adaptation to the American negotiating style (many Israelis have attended courses on the subject, some of which focus on styles and schools of thought popular in the U.S.)

- the stage in the process

- the situation

That is, is it a one-time-only deal or the first step in

building a long-term relationship? Are there two sets of negotiators, each of which contains several individuals, or is one individual facing a group? Is the setting a formal meeting, as it was in "First Impressions," or more informal? What's being negotiated? Nevertheless, and despite the variations these factors cause, it is legitimate to speak of an Israeli style with general characteristics or tendencies.

As we've seen, Israelis are uncomfortable with formality, ceremony, and protocol. This is frequently true of Americans as well, but the threshold of Israeli discomfort is lower. As a result, they tend to rush through the icebreaking or relationship-building stage of the negotiation process at a faster pace than Americans are accustomed to. They spend relatively little time on introductions and small talk and often may appear to be just going through the motions. Israelis want to get down to the business at hand. The transition from formality (maintaining one's distance) to informality (bridging the distance) also occurs at a relatively rapid pace. American negotiators may feel, as the chairperson felt in "First Impressions," that the Israelis act as if they've known the Americans for years when, in fact, they've been talking to each other for only a few hours.

Functioning in their fast-forward modes, many Israelis enter into a negotiation with the expectation that events will proceed at a rapid pace. They might even expect an initial meeting to end in a deal and may express their disappointment when it doesn't. Americans, on the other hand, tend to approach an initial meeting with the expectation that it will result, at best, in breaking the ice—getting to know one's negotiating partners—and exchanging information.

A curious dichotomy seems to exist in Israeli relationship building. If the icebreaking takes place in a formal setting, it will usually be perfunctory. However, if a relationship develops outside of the work environment, Israelis may tend to assume that the chemistry that has been created will carry more weight in the formal negotiation process than it actually does. Here's where the unclear demarcation between professional and personal self and the Israeli penchant for boundary crossing may cause misunderstandings. The American inclination is to draw clear lines between work and play. In negotiations, this often expresses itself in a tendency to put personal relationships aside and to consider the issues primarily on the basis of their merit.

The Israeli communication style can sometimes be an irritant in the negotiation process. Americans may well find that Israeli directness, forcefulness, and confrontation cause friction and make it difficult for the negotiating partners to establish an atmosphere of cooperation. On the other hand, American negotiators may welcome Israeli directness. Their message comes across loud and clear even if it sometimes has a rough, sandpapery quality.

Israeli negotiators often have a problem figuring out what American negotiators really mean. The problem stems in part from the less direct American communication style—"I think I might have a problem with that," "I'm not sure that I agree." However, it also stems from cultural differences centering around the meaning of the word "no." When Americans say "No, that's completely impossible," the meaning is almost always unequivocal. When Israelis say "No, that's completely impossible," it often means: "I'm starting off tough. I'll say this. Now, let's hear what you're going to say." In other words, no doesn't always mean no. The result: Israelis will often continue to push a point or to negotiate when Americans feel they've made it clear that the discussion is closed. Americans, on the other hand, often hear the Israeli no and assume that the bargaining process has come to an end. Sometimes, they miss out on important opportunities.

Other components of the Israeli communication style may prove distracting and make it difficult for Americans to concentrate. Among Israelis, there is a tendency to speak in conversational overlaps, that is, to start their sentence before the other person finishes his or hers. In practical terms, this means that one can expect to be interrupted and to witness Israelis interrupting each other (see "An Informal Discussion" on page 116). Israelis also seem to be able to tolerate situations in which several things are happening at once. Meetings in Israel are frequently interrupted by telephone calls and people dropping in to deliver messages or ask questions.

Israeli inattention to hierarchy may also influence how negotiations are carried on. If you are meeting with an Israeli team, you may discover that junior members of the team, particularly if they are specialists in certain areas, may contradict senior members in your presence. Since Americans are less likely to behave in this manner, you may erroneously conclude that the senior negotiator lacks authority. If Israeli inattention to hierarchy expresses itself in behavior toward you, you may have a different reaction. For instance, you may be quite annoyed when, after stating your teams's "no" in polite but unequivocal terms, an Israeli turns to your subordinates and asks them what they think—especially if in an off-the-record conversation they've discovered that the thinking of junior members of your team differs from yours.

If you are a woman on an American team, cultural differences centering around gender relationships will probably affect the behavior of the Israelis toward you. Since there tend to be fewer women on corporate negotiating teams in Israel than there are in the U.S., you may find that you have to work three times as hard as your male counterparts to be taken seriously. (In the U.S., you may only have to work twice as hard!) There may be instances in which Israeli men compliment you in a manner you consider patronizing—"Wow, are you good!"—when it would never occur to them to compliment a man who was simply performing his job competently. You may also find that both Israeli men and women are more comfortable with flirting in the workplace than their American counterparts. (See chapter 3 for more on gender relationships in Israel.)

One of the most important cultural issues influencing cross-cultural negotiations is the participants' definitions of trust and that which is trustworthy. Indeed, this may be the issue on which everything hinges. *Americans tend to trust other people until they prove themselves untrustworthy. Israelis tend to distrust other people until they prove themselves trustworthy.*

There is no way that the importance of this cultural difference can be underestimated. It affects every stage of the negotiating process; in fact, it affects the way in which the negotiating process itself is viewed and the manner in which American and Israeli negotiators view each other (see "Differences at a Glance," page 83). And it doesn't matter whether one is negotiating a multimillion dollar business agreement or the purchase of a new stereo system. (In Israel, prices on appliances in stores may be marked, but they are, nevertheless, frequently negotiable.)

According to most generally accepted models of the negotiation process, agreeing on procedure and exchanging task-related information usually follow the icebreaking or relationship-building stage. In the agreeing-on-procedure stage, Americans tend to lay their cards on the table and be relatively open about their goals. They are usually willing to devote considerable time to understanding the background and interests of the other side and making sure that the other side understands theirs. The implicit assumption is that an exchange of task-related information and agreement on procedure can minimize misunderstandings and maximize efficiency. It can also contribute to a climate of agreement and cooperation and, ideally, trust.

Israelis are far less trusting. Suspecting that the other side has hidden as well as stated goals and that any information revealed can be used to their disadvantage, they tend to play their cards close to the chest and to reveal as little as possible regarding their own intentions.

The phrase "respect them and suspect them" summarizes the Israeli approach to the opening stages of the negotiation process. Israelis *are* willing to invest time and energy to create a cooperative climate and the necessary trust to continue negotiations. However, for Israelis such a climate isn't something that can be taken for granted. If one's cultural tendency is to distrust the other side, then one would reasonably expect a climate of disagreement and confrontation rather than agreement and cooperation.

Israeli negotiators often express a desire to move as quickly as possible from the stage of agreeing on procedure and exchanging information to the bidding and bargaining stages. During the bargaining process, Israelis will often adopt a confrontational style ("That's totally impossible!") instead of a more open style ("Let me explain why that's a problem for us.") In fact, their behavior may indicate that they view the negotiation as a contest of wills in which the side that is tougher and holds out longer gets the better deal. When Americans are involved in persuading and bargaining, they tend to offer remarks in the form of suggestions rather than ultimatums and to explain their rationale for espousing a particular point of view. Acting in this manner, it is believed, will make both sides more conciliatory and will foster an atmosphere conducive to arriving at a fair agreement. Being reasonable is a high priority. Israelis are less concerned about being (or seeming) reasonable than they are about achieving their goal.

When it comes to concessions and agreements, Americans tend to be more comfortable with a win-win approach than Israelis are. The assumption behind win-win is that it is possible to reach agreements which meet the legitimate interests of each side and resolve conflicting interests fairly. Because they are less trusting than Americans to begin with, Israelis tend to believe that win-lose is a closer reflection of reality. The Israeli subtext may very well be: "If you say that we've reached a win-win solution, what you really mean is that you've gotten everything you wanted and you want me to think that I've come away with something too, when in fact I've come away on the losing end." Of course, in the face of an evident win-lose attitude, Americans may become just as suspicious, mistrustful, and tough as their Israeli counterparts.

We do not mean to imply that all Israeli negotiators adopt a win-lose approach or that all American negotiators adopt a win-win approach. There is as much variation in the American style as there is in the Israeli one, and there are times when the styles overlap.

Any discussion of Israeli-American cultural differences centering around the issue of trust has to be seen in a broader context. All cultures can be placed on a continuum from basic trust to basic distrust of others. Americans tend to be on the extreme "trust" end of the continuum. In other words, relative to Americans not only Israelis but virtually all other cultures are far less trusting. Israeli negotiators have far more in common with negotiators from Europe, the Middle East, Asia, Africa, and South America on this cultural parameter than they do with negotiators from the United States. This assessment should not be misread, however. Americans will negotiate as hard as anyone else to reach agreements which satisfy their own self-interest.

8

The Choreography of the Social Dance

"Let's Get Together Sometime!"

Gabi, an Israeli man on a three-year assignment in the U.S., describes a social encounter with an American:

> After a corporate assignment in Europe, it was a pleasure, at first, to be in the United States. The Europeans had been closed, distant, and formal. A "Good morning, sir," at the elevator was the closest our neighbors had come to breaking the ice. They certainly hadn't spared any time initiating conversations with strangers. In fact, we had always felt like strangers—frozen out!
>
> Americans, on the other hand, seemed to be more open, and certainly more friendly. I've never seen a country with so many smiling people. Smiles in the supermarket, smiles on airplanes, smiles when people make eye contact, smiles at social gatherings between people who have never met. We were on a first-name basis almost immediately. They spoke casually: "Hi! How ya doin'?"; "It's nice to meet you"; "Let's get together sometime!"
>
> Now that we've been in the U.S. for three months, however, I've become sick and tired of their smiles and "friendliness." I've come to the conclusion that they say all of these

151

things without meaning them. In fact, I'm convinced that there is something hypocritical in their conviviality. They aren't interested in being friends. They simply talk a good game. Sometimes, though, I'm not sure how to interpret their behavior. Here's an example:

My eight-year-old son has joined the basketball league sponsored by the Jewish Community Center. Like all the other parents, I've become an enthusiastic fan and go with him to all the games. A few weeks ago, during a Sunday afternoon game, I sat next to Phil, the father of one of the American kids on the team. We chatted for at least an hour. I guess you could call it "small talk." He seemed like a nice guy. We talked about our kids and our work in Washington. Basketball, of course, also figured in the discussion.

When the kids finished playing and were ready to go home, he turned to me and said:

"It was great talking to you." I murmured something like, "Same here." Phil's response: "Let's get together sometime. Maybe I can get tickets for a basketball game."

I'd been burnt before, so I didn't want to make a fool of myself by letting him think that I had taken him seriously. But I couldn't be sure; maybe he really meant what he said. So I mumbled something like "OK" in a noncommittal tone. He made no attempt to pursue the conversation or to persist in his efforts to persuade me to go with him to a game. I'm almost positive that he was just being polite and had no real intention of initiating a friendship. On the other hand....

We've deliberately presented "Let's Get Together Sometime" from an Israeli perspective. Gabi's response is an example of a communication breakdown resulting from significant cultural differences. Is it possible that American friendliness is hurtful? How can people be put off by a smile? Can small talk be misleading? Why is politeness sometimes perceived as hypocrisy? If we look at the behavior through Israeli eyes, we can begin to understand Gabi's reaction.

Initially, Gabi's thoughts ran as follows: "Americans seem friendly. Israelis are friendly. Americans appear to be informal. Israelis are informal. When Israelis are friendly, it's because they're genuinely interested. Therefore, I can assume that when Americans are friendly, they're also genuinely interested. I can relax and feel at home."

Exposure to American friendliness over the course of three months, however, produced a different set of conclusions. Gabi encountered that friendliness—casual small talk, smiles, first names, "Hi! How ya doin'?"—in a number of settings: the supermarket, airport, parent-teacher meetings, informal social gatherings, and sports events like the basketball game in the incident. In most cases, the friendly demeanor seemed to be an end in itself. It didn't lead to friendships as it would in Israel. For Israelis, the American behavior was a tease leading to disappointment.

Gabi was convinced that the Americans were sending contradictory signals. They were transmitting openness and friendliness in their first responses, while their subsequent behavior indicated they were closed and unfriendly. His difficulty stemmed, in part, from his inability to distinguish between friendliness as courtesy and friendliness as an attempt to initiate a relationship.

An American would be able to read between the lines, respond accordingly, and interpret the codes. "Let's get together sometime" was followed by "Maybe I can get tickets for a basketball game." The American, Phil, had moved beyond mere politeness and was waiting for the response that is part of the American "social dance."

The choreography of this dance consisted of taking a step forward: "It was great talking to you" (polite end of conversation) and waiting for a response. Gabi then took a step forward: "Same here." Phil advanced another step and made a little sideways motion too. "Maybe I can get tickets for a basketball game" (general commitment; a move beyond politeness) and waited for Gabi's response. Gabi didn't dance. Instead of answering with a pleased "I'd like that," he replied with a phlegmatic "OK." It appeared to Phil that his partner wasn't interested in dancing. Phil stepped back. Pushing the issue would be inappropriate. He didn't want to intrude or be rebuffed.

A Few Words about the Ubiquitous American Smile

The famous American smile compounds Gabi's difficulties in interpreting American behavior. Gabi tells us that he's never met so many smiling people. Europeans make this observation as well. Americans grow up with spots on television saying "Smile. It makes your face feel good." Mothers tell their daughters: "You're prettier when you smile." People who don't smile are viewed as impolite. Smiling is part of friendliness, and friendliness is a component of politeness.

Like other Israelis who came before him, Gabi first interpreted the smiles as friendliness. Israelis smile only when they want to or someone's behavior causes them to do so. A smile is a genuine response to a specific person or situation. It signals a readiness to engage in social or sexual interaction. Once Gabi realized that the clerk who smiled at him was also smiling at everyone else in line at the supermarket, or the woman at the cocktail party who smiled at him smiled at everyone else in the same way, he naturally concluded that the American smile is an artifice. It's automatic. It loses value for him, because everybody gets one.

Gabi's confusion can also be explained by his lack of familiarity with small talk as it is carried on in the United States. As discussed in previous chapters, Israeli society is distinguished by its informality. The ceremonial aspects of social interaction are kept to a minimum and are often viewed as artificial.

This is not to say that Israelis who are curious or interested in initiating a conversation never engage in small talk. It simply takes a different form: "Where are you from? Haifa? You went to the Reali High School. So did a good friend of mine from the army. Oh, you know Avi? I thought so...." In other words, Israelis quickly discover that they have mutual friends or acquaintances.

Americans are known for their mobility, the degree to which they not only travel constantly but move their place of residence with striking frequency. They continuously find themselves in social situations where everyone is a stranger and where making substantial personal connections is both very difficult and emotionally wearing. American small talk, then, often revolves around subjects likely to be within everyone's frame of reference, e.g., weather or sports.

In Israel, people don't move their place of residence as frequently as they do in the United States; and even if they do, the country is so small that they can't really move far enough to be in a place where they don't know anyone. Israelis, therefore, have little occasion to develop the skills in initiating and carrying on a conversation with someone who is a complete stranger and with whom they don't personally connect in some way.

It would be a mistake to conclude, however, that Israelis are unfriendly. On the contrary. Israeli spontaneity allows individuals who are naturally open or motivated by curiosity, physical attraction, or genuine human warmth to initiate a conversation with a stranger quite easily.

Adapting to the Situation

The above discussion has, of course, practical implications for American newcomers to Israel:

1. When Americans realize how Israelis interpret their smiles, many jump to the conclusion that smiling is out. Not so. You can smile with the same frequency and in the same circumstances that you smile in the U.S. Simply realize that your smile may sometimes be misinterpreted. You may be perceived as artificial, or your smile may be perceived as a sexual come-on. On

156

the other hand, you can try not to smile so automatically or reflexively. Let your smiles bubble up spontaneously and reflect special feelings about specific people or a particular situation. And don't be offended if Israelis don't smile automatically at you. The smiles will come in due course.

2. Remember that an automatic "Let's get together sometime," devoid of intent to pursue the matter, touches an Israeli nerve. If you are genuinely interested in initiating a friendship, you might want to add a sentence like "I really mean it." Be specific. The reverse is also important. When Israelis invite you to their homes, they usually mean it. "Why don't you drop in this Shabbat" is a real invitation. If you politely say "OK" or "I'll try," the Israelis will be expecting you and will be hurt if you do not show up.

3. If you are engaging an Israeli in small talk and he or she seems to be unresponsive, try not to interpret the behavior as rudeness or lack of interest. The individual may simply be unaccustomed to that particular social ritual, or at least to the manner in which the ritual of getting to know someone is carried out in the U.S.

The previous incident was described from an Israeli point of view. The following social interaction is described from the *American* standpoint.

"In America, We Don't Ask Those Questions."

The incident is related by Maggie. She and her husband are in Israel on a two-year assignment with an Israeli social service organization.

Last Shabbat, we were invited to the Cohens's home for coffee. We were touched by their warmth and hospitality. After all, we had been in the apartment for just a week. The

Cohens seemed interested in every aspect of our lives and asked a lot of questions: "How are the children getting along at school? Do you miss your family? Are you thinking of immigrating? Are you planning to buy an apartment or continue renting? That's a lovely blouse. Did you buy it here? Do you mind telling me how much you paid for it?" They even asked questions about our income and possessions: "How much did you pay for the TV? For your video? How much will you be making as an English teacher? How does it compare with what you were earning as a teacher in California?" My husband seemed a little shell-shocked by the "interrogation," but he answered their questions. I kept quiet, but finally, I couldn't take it any longer. I simply said, "In America, we don't ask those questions." Afterwards, I said to my husband, "It's obvious that they have no concept of privacy!"

Judging by her response, it is clear that Maggie was offended by the Cohens's questions. She viewed them as an invasion of privacy, particularly since the Cohens were only new acquaintances. According to Israeli norms, however, the Cohens were simply expressing curiosity. One's income and how much one paid for something are regarded in Israel as acceptable subjects of conversation. In the U.S. they are not.

Israelis are also freer in discussing other subjects which Americans tend to shy away from. Politics and religion are the two most prominent. For Americans, discussing politics and religion risks conflict and confrontation. For many Israelis, argument and confrontation are enjoyable, something to be welcomed rather than avoided. They are ways of "keeping in social shape"—sparring, arguing, testing, taking a stand, working things out.

The American communication style is characterized by the avoidance of open confrontation, especially at an early stage in a relationship. Being friendly means being "nice" or "polite," which includes not being argumentative.

Adapting to the Situation

Our central theme of border crossings expresses itself in American-Israeli social interactions. Israelis tend to ask questions which seem intrusive to Americans, i.e., overstepping the boundary between private and public, and to cross over into forbidden areas, e.g., politics, which violate American conversational taboos. How do you deal with these differences in your interactions with Israelis? Here are a few practical tips:

If Israelis ask you how much you paid for something or how much money you are making, and you don't want to reveal the information, you can respond as Maggie did. Or you can try to view questions about prices and income as expressions of curiosity rather than intrusiveness. In either case, you have several options:

1. You can explain, without making a judgment: "I'm kind of uncomfortable with those kinds of questions. We're not used to them in the United States, though we probably ask questions that make you uncomfortable too."

2. You can answer in general terms, perhaps even humorously. If the question is "How much are you paying in rent?" you can reply "A lot."

3. You can, of course, change the subject.

4. You may decide to answer certain questions—e.g., how much you paid for your television—and not answer others—e.g., those about income.

5. You can adopt a "when in Rome..." attitude and simply answer all questions, even if you view them as an intrusion of privacy.

6. Expect the process of getting to know someone to occur at a relatively rapid pace. Individuals may bring up subjects you regard as controversial when you feel that you're just getting acquainted. If your host or

hostess brings up a subject taboo in an American social setting, feel free to speak up. It's okay to argue even if it's your first visit. You might even find it enjoyable! If you are uncomfortable on fast-forward, however, pull back and refrain from getting into an argument until you know the people better. This may occur in another twenty minutes or another two months.

If you do find yourself getting into an argument, try not to be intimidated by the Israeli confrontational style. No one is angry with you, or anyone else, for that matter. Things may seem out of control, but they're usually not.

If you're a woman, expect to be at a disadvantage in the Darwinian struggle to make yourself heard. In a culture which is noisy and loud, those with the louder voices (men) will tend to dominate the discussion.

7. It would be a mistake to conclude that Israelis welcome an argument on virtually any issue. There are subjects that Israelis are sensitive about and there is one topic, in particular, that we suggest you approach with extreme caution. It touches a nerve in the collective Israeli psyche.

Israelis are usually delighted to discuss the army or even to argue about the army in the context of politics. If, however, an outsider suggests that the actions of Israeli soldiers vis-à-vis the Arabs in the territories can be compared to the actions of the Nazis during the Holocaust, there will be an extreme reaction. Many Israelis are survivors of the Holocaust; others are children or grandchildren of Holocaust survivors. Every Israeli, regardless of ethnic background, studies the Holocaust in school and comes to view it as a part of the collective Jewish historical experience. For Israelis, nothing whatsoever is equivalent to the Holocaust, certainly not the actions of Jewish soldiers.

Just as it would be a mistake to conclude that there are no subjects about which Israelis are sensitive, it would also be a mistake to conclude that Israelis have no sense of privacy. Israelis and Americans simply have different views about which issues are considered private. While Israelis don't seem to have the kinds of specific conversational taboos Americans do, they do have a general taboo on self-disclosure to people who are not close friends. In an earlier incident we discussed Maggie's response to the Cohens's questions about money-related issues. Two years later, the following incident was reported by Daphna Cohen. Maggie's former neighbors had just returned from a sabbatical in the United States.

"We Weren't Sure If They Expected Us to Respond."

After being burned by our experience with our American neighbors in Israel, we learned that Americans are very sensitive about discussing certain issues. Since we certainly had no wish to offend anyone, we vowed never again to ask Americans about income or the cost of their possessions.

A few months after our arrival in the U.S., we were invited to the home of two of our colleagues at the university. During the course of the evening, they revealed the following information: it was the second marriage for both of them; Alice, the hostess, was recovering from a traumatic bout with lung cancer; their two teenaged children were in psychotherapy; a close friend had died of AIDS.

We both were embarrassed by the degree of self-revelation. We weren't sure if they expected us to respond by divulging details of our private lives. That, of course, was an impossibility. Avi and I would have to know someone for years before we'd reveal such personal information. These Americans are really strange. They are terribly offended if you ask a harmless question about income, but within forty-five minutes of meeting you, they'll voluntarily relate the most intimate personal details.

What is private and what is not is a key issue in the case described above. For the American couple, subjects like divorce, cancer, AIDS, and psychotherapy clearly did *not* fall under the category of subjects one does not discuss. For Daphna and Avi, they did. Self-disclosure of this kind seems to make Israelis feel uncomfortable. We don't presume to know all the reasons. Perhaps it has something to do with the smallness of the country.

In the 1990s, everyone at a party may not know everyone else, as they would have a generation ago, but each person will probably be able to identify at least one mutual acquaintance. Unless one is talking with close friends one has known for years (and even then, sometimes), the "We're all from the same small town" frame of reference expresses itself in a hesitancy to talk about subjects that will increase one's vulnerability. The probability is high that one will run into the same person or have mutual acquaintances. A spicy disclosure will certainly be shared.

Cultural differences between Americans and Israelis about privacy don't have to do only with discussion topics and personal questions. They also concern the manner in which individuals relate to a group. Israeli culture is group-oriented. Interestingly, the collectivity of Israeli society is reflected in its movies, which are often about groups of people—classmates, army buddies, or a gang of friends. No one person functions as a main character.[1]

Consider the following scenes:

- As a privacy-loving American, you look for a campsite in the wilderness. You want to get away from it all, to reconnect with your family and nature. Within minutes of setting up your tent, however, you find yourself surrounded by a convoy of four cars filled with happy,

---

[1] Stuart Schoffman, "Write It Again, Shmulik," *Jerusalem Report,* 9 April 1992, 35.

noisy Israeli families, all busily engaged in putting up their tents. Why?

The other families assume that you must have found a wonderful site and will be delighted to share it. They, of course, will be pleased to share their equipment, food, tools, and kids' toys with you. They are completely baffled by the unhappy expression on your face. If you decide to pack up and go elsewhere, they will be hurt and upset.

- Your host at the plant has invited you to a party at his home. You are excited and wary, but you decide to test the water. Cautious about plunging into a social scene with which you are unfamiliar, you would be perfectly happy to find a quiet corner, be an observer for a while, and perhaps get into a conversation with one or two people. But it doesn't work that way. You discover that there are no quiet corners. The furniture has been arranged in a large single circle where you are expected to sit while engaging in intense conversation with several people at once.

Here you seem to be sucked into a vortex but it is, in reality, just the benign Israeli group-seating arrangement. You sense a set of contradictions. On the one hand, the conversation is lively and dynamic. People are talking about topics they really care about. There is a lot of energy in the air. On the other hand, there is very little movement around the room. You are seated in the same chair throughout most of the evening and notice that others are, too. You finally figure it out. You are accustomed to an American party pattern: a series of conversations in small groups. People change seats as the small groups change, and they move from place to place around the room. Sometimes everyone is standing to begin with, and they circulate for an entire evening. In Israel, you discover, the dominant communication pattern is between the individual and the *entire group*. From your seat, you may be participating in the "main theme" conversation/debate involving everyone present, plus at least two small conversations—to your right, left, and perhaps the opposite side of the circle—simultaneously.

All of the incidents discussed thus far concern the early stages of building a relationship. What happens when one overcomes the initial cultural barriers and develops a friendship with an Israeli? Misunderstandings, if they exist at all, stem from different expectations of someone in the role of friend.

Israelis distinguish among stranger, acquaintance, casual friend (*yadeed* in Hebrew), and close friend (*chaver*). Casual friends may visit each others' homes or go to the movies together. They may play tennis or basketball. Close friends have usually known each other for a long time and have often been part of each other's personal history. Close friendship is a bond carrying mutual commitment and obligation. Close friends are expected to help each other without worrying about being intrusive or causing inconvenience.

Americans tend to use the word "friend" to refer to anyone along the scale from a passing acquaintance to someone with whom one plays tennis to a lifetime intimate. They do distinguish between friends (or close friends) and acquaintances, but the loose usage of the terms can be confusing to non-Americans. Friends are certainly expected to do favors that mere acquaintances would not (putting you up for the night if you are passing through town, for instance). One is expected to "be there" for one's friends, but one also has to be careful not to be intrusive or to make too many demands on their time.

American self-sufficiency is an issue here as well. In the United States, asking for help somehow diminishes one's sense of self-worth. Leaning on others, including one's friends, is not considered quite legitimate. If I can't do it myself, I am in some way inadequate, in my own eyes as well as those of my friends.

As noted in the metaphor discussion in chapter 4, Israelis also value self-sufficiency. That's why they have difficulty turning to professionals, institutions, or people they don't know for help. Israelis assigned to the United States on relocation, for example, often go through the hassle of finding an apartment on their own rather than seeking professional guidance from a real-estate agent. However, it is legitimate to lean on one's close friends. The bonds of friendship take priority over the need for self-sufficiency.

Adapting to the Situation

If you want to speed up the adaptation process and move along more quickly in the direction of Israeli norms, try dropping over to someone else's house without a great deal of advance notice—in the same way as they are apt to drop in on you. Feel free to ask Israeli friends for just about any favor. You don't have to think that you are intruding or that you "owe them one." Israelis are hurt by this expression when it is used among friends.

Your Israeli friends will, in turn, expect you to go out of your way for them. This may mean that you'll have to think about reorganizing your priorities. Here's an example: You have to participate in an important meeting at work. Your friend, who is sick but not in critical condition, needs your help to get to the hospital. That means that you'll be late for the meeting. In terms of Israeli cultural norms, taking your friend to the hospital assumes first priority. Your Israeli colleagues at work will accept your decision. They may delay the start of the meeting so that you can participate.

Conclusion

In the choreography of the social dance, the misunderstandings begin with the American approach: Is friendliness simple courtesy, or is it an invitation to the dance, a signal that someone is interested in initiating a friendship? Once the social dance begins, the two partners often discover that they

are dancing to different music. Coordination becomes difficult, and the dance is awkward. Both partners may ask themselves, "What dance is this, anyway?" Israeli spontaneity
sometimes clashes with American reserve, and American
spontaneity sometimes conflicts with Israeli reserve.

In part, the clash occurs because of differences in communication style. Israelis tend to prefer conversations that contain an element of friendly confrontation; in the early stages
of a social interaction, Americans tend to be more comfortable avoiding confrontation. However, the more significant
issue is privacy. To Americans, it seems that Israelis lack a
filtering mechanism. They seem to bring up subjects spontaneously and ask questions without first asking themselves
whether they are intruding on someone else's privacy or
causing an embarrassing confrontation. Israelis, on the other
hand, are often embarrassed by the spontaneous manner with
which Americans volunteer information about subjects Israelis regard as private. Each partner feels that the other is
violating personal space, crossing a boundary into an area
marked "keep out" or "enter with caution."

The cultural differences discussed above are certainly irritants. Sometimes they are minor—one misses a few steps in
the social dance. At other times, they are major—one wants
to walk away. However, once one has gotten beyond the
initial misunderstandings in social interactions and sur-
mounted the early obstacles to friendship building, simple
chemistry or common interests usually take over. And in
social interactions with Israelis, you have a greater choice
than you do in other interactions. In commercial, bureaucratic, or professional settings, there are certain individuals
with whom you *must* interact. In social relationships, you
have the luxury of picking and choosing until you find the
individuals with whom you are most comfortable.

Afterword

We've divided the book into separate chapters on commercial/bureaucratic, professional, and social interactions. These divisions are a necessary device for describing the components of Israeli culture. In doing so, however, we have contradicted our central theme: borders in Israel are loosely defined. The boundaries between professional, commercial, and social arenas are blurred, as are those inside the arenas: clients and vendors, managers and subordinates, hosts and guests, strangers and friends. Ill-defined borders are easier to cross than those which are sharply delineated. Israelis find it difficult to stay within clearly defined limits because, in Israel, they hardly exist.

Not only are borders blurred, other things in Israel are as well. If the country is secular and religious, Western and Middle Eastern, melting pot, salad bowl, and pressure cooker, what happens to the American visitor accustomed to roles and situations which are more clearly defined?

At first glance, it seems the answer should be obvious. Ambiguity and fuzzy borders often cause intense frustration for American sojourners. Israeli border crossings—challenges to authority, violations of personal space, breaching of taboos, forays into other people's professional territory, self-

167

confidence expressed in a forceful and confrontational communication style—can bring Americans to the point where they say "Why bother?" or "Why would any American want to be engaged in ongoing interactions with Israelis?"

Interestingly enough, the answer isn't obvious at all. Many Americans discover that they're drawn to Israel precisely because of its ambiguities and fuzzy boundaries. Or they are repelled and attracted at the same time. Continuous border crossings—on-the-spot improvisational problem solving, spontaneous changing of plans, moving fast in professional and social relationships—produce a society with a very high energy level. There's little predictability and many surprises. Things are exciting, always in motion. Since there are few barriers to hold people back, there is an immediacy and intensity in personal relationships.

Of course, culture shock still rears its annoying and often very ugly head, even for Americans whose reaction to Israel is overwhelmingly positive. Although there is no way of eliminating culture shock, there are ways of softening it. We believe that *Border Crossings* provides you with a set of reasonable expectations regarding both Israel and yourself. Will it enable you to suspend judgment? To conclude that there are no better or worse cultures, just different ones? Probably not. Professional anthropologists are sometimes able to suspend judgment. Americans interacting with Israelis usually don't. There's too much that's sandpapery, little that's cushioned, and it's all whizzing by in fast-forward.

We hope that our book will enable you to monitor, rather than suspend, judgment. You're going to like some things and not like others, label certain behaviors funny, rude, unprofessional, admirable. And then you're going to glance in the cultural mirror we've provided and be reminded that Israelis are looking at you and labeling your American behavior in ways which may well be at odds with your view of yourself.

As cultural guides, we have provided some signposts. We invite you to make your own journey.

Appendix A

Coping-Strategies Exercise for Commercial Transactions and Bureaucratic Encounters

Newcomers in Israel daily experience "cultural dissonance," i.e., the disorientation of confronting behaviors and norms at odds with their American expectations. The question then becomes: "How should one respond?" To what extent should one attempt to adapt one's behavior to Israeli expectations?

Total adaptation to Israeli culture, indeed, to any new culture, is rare. Most immigrants, including those who've made a conscious effort to transform themselves into Israelis, discover this after many years in the country. The difficulty is even greater for a visitor, who has less time and probably less motivation to adapt fully to Israeli society. Nevertheless, if one is going to be effective in pursuing whatever one's goals are in Israel, some degree of adaptation is imperative. The issue is not *whether* one will adapt, but how much and under what circumstances. The following incident provides the basis for an exercise which will enable you to explore the range of responses in commercial transactions and bureaucratic encounters.

169

"I Lost Control!"

Bob, a physician on a two-year sabbatical in Israel, relates the following incident:

It was August. I took time off from a very busy hospital schedule to go up to Haifa from Tel Aviv. My car had arrived in the port and I wanted to take care of all the necessary paperwork as quickly as possible. I traveled from Tel Aviv to Haifa in a non-air-conditioned bus—my luck! I arrived at the customs house by 8:30 A.M. There were already at least forty people ahead of me. My turn came at 10:00. I was tired and impatient, but relieved. If all my papers were in order, I would be out of the customs area by 10:30. I sat down in the empty chair opposite the clerk. However, his agenda proved to be different from mine. He said, "hafsaka" (coffee break). Joined by all the other workers in the office, he got up and announced that work would resume at 10:30.

Another worker taking another coffee break. This was too much. I lost control! I found myself reaching over the desk, putting my hands on his shirt collar and saying: "I'm a doctor. I know how to break your neck. If you don't process my papers right this minute, I'm going to kill you!" He was so startled by this non-American, uncivilized behavior that he didn't even call the police. Instead, he processed my papers and I returned from Haifa with my new car. I should have been overjoyed. Instead, I was in shock. I realized that Freud was right. The veneer of civilization is very thin. I had lost control, reverted to behavior totally out of character, indeed, unacceptable. I'll do anything to avoid repeating that scene.

The following exercise is designed to prevent the stress-produced reaction described above. Examining the full range of options beforehand will increase the probability that you will act in ways which are effective in Israel and appropriate for you.

We've used this exercise in orientation workshops for Americans going to Israel or engaged in ongoing contact with Israelis. We make no claims for its scientific or statistical validity, but we do know that it's proved a useful tool that reveals as much about personality as it does about culture. It's also enjoyable if done in a group where participants compare their responses and discuss the implications. There's usually a lot of laughter. People turn to each other saying, "You'd do *that?* I can't believe it!"

Below begins a list of coping strategies arranged on a scale from low-key/nonconfrontational to confrontational/aggressive.

Go back and reread "I Lost Control!" or review some of the incidents described in chapter 5. Choose one of them. For example, take "Trying to See the Doctor" and imagine yourself in the same situation.

Next, study the coping-strategy menu to familiarize yourself with the great range of ways people can respond to cross-cultural incidents.

The Coping-Strategy Menu for Commercial Transactions and Bureaucratic Encounters:

1. Withdraw

2. Withdraw temporarily (return with a friend or veteran coper)

3. Straightforwardly explain your problem in a business-like manner

4. Show willingness to compromise

5. Smile

6. Display empathy

7. Use the name of a friend or acquaintance ("Ilan told me to see you.")

8. Evoke sympathy for your plight

9. Elicit curiosity about yourself or your history

10. Play dumb

11. Appeal to the other person's sense of humor

12. Exaggerate your situation

13. Evoke pity

14. Appeal to the audience (the other customers, patients, etc.)

15. Flatter

16. Flirt

17. Impose guilt

18. Grovel

19. Cry

20. Insist on seeing the person in authority

21. Threaten to report him or her to a higher authority (boss, head office)

22. Rreport to higher authority

23. Refuse to leave until you get what you came for

24. Raise your voice

25. Shout

26. Threaten to give him or her a bad reputation with other customers

27. Threaten damage to property

28. Damage property

29. Threaten personal injury

30. Cause personal injury

A Few Words of Explanation

Following are brief explanations of items on the menu which may be unclear:

1. withdraw: simply get up and leave.

6. display empathy: "I can imagine how annoying it must be to hear the same story day after day."

8. evoke sympathy for your plight: "I know that the office is officially closed, but I got stuck in a traffic jam on the way from Jerusalem."

9. elicit curiosity about yourself or your history: "You probably don't get too many customers who grew up in Hawaii."

10. play dumb: "I didn't know I had to come early to get a number to see the doctor. All the signs are in Hebrew and I'm only in the beginners' class."

14. appeal to the audience: turn to the other patients in the presence of the nurse, evoke sympathy for your plight, and get them to intercede on your behalf.

17. impose guilt: "Aren't you ashamed? You say that you welcome tourists and this is the way you act!"

18. grovel: "Please, please, please, let me in to see the doctor!"

Now do the following:

1. Place a Y (Yes) next to the coping strategies you feel comfortable with and/or use now as a visitor, prospective visitor, or someone in the U.S. engaged in ongoing contact with Israelis. (Or, if you have had no experience with Israelis, place a Y next to the coping strategies you feel comfortable with and/or use now in American commercial and bureaucratic encounters.)

2. Place an M (Maybe) next to the coping strategies you might feel comfortable using three months from now.

(Three months is not an arbitrary time period. It is long enough to form an impression of behavior patterns and gain some idea of how things work and what strategies are effective; yet it is too short a period to understand the reasons for the behavior or to internalize unfamiliar norms.)

(If you are reading this chapter before your first exposure to Israelis or your first visit to Israel, place an M next to the coping strategies you *think* you would feel comfortable using after three months.)

3. Place an N (No) next to the coping strategies you believe you could not and would not ever use. These are the strategies which you feel may compromise your integrity. You may even find them morally abhorrent or perhaps just repugnant or strongly uncharacteristic of your personality.

4. Count and record the number of Y's, M's and N's. Look for clusters, e.g., groups of one answer in some section of the menu.

5. Complete these sentences:

"Right now, I feel comfortable using strategies which can be described as...":

Choose from the following list:
  low-key
  businesslike/professional
  dramatic
  confrontational
  manipulative
  nonconfrontational
  other

"In three months (or three months after my arrival in Israel), I may feel comfortable using strategies which can be described as...":

Choose again from the above list.

Instructions for group work:

1. Compare and record responses to each item. For example, next to item 1—(withdraw)—your group may list responses *YNMY*.

2. Identify items around which consensus—unanimous responses—exists: *YYYY, MMMM, or NNNN*.

3. Attempt to determine why this consensus has occurred. Can it be explained, for example, by American cultural norms?

4. How do you explain the differences among members of your group? For example, is willingness to use coping strategies like "Demanding to See the Manager" (item 20) or "Flirting" a function of gender, length of time in Israel, mastery of Hebrew, age, etc.?

The strategies listed at the beginning of the numerical scale (1-5) are relatively low-key: reserved, nonconfrontational, and impersonal. Strategies 6-19 can be described as increasingly dramatic and personal. They require less inhibition and a greater willingness to call attention to oneself. Strategies 20-25 are confrontational, while strategies 26-30 can be described as both confrontational and aggressive.

If your Y's clustered in the beginning of the scale, it is clear that at the present time, you are most comfortable with behaviors consistent with the American communication style. The same holds true if your Y's clustered toward the end of the scale (20-21, confrontational but businesslike and controlled). The American communication style places a premium on maintaining self-control and on preserving the distinction between personal and professional self.

If your M's are clustered in the middle of the scale (6-19), we can safely assume that you're ready to try out behaviors more prevalent in Israel. These strategies call for a relative lack of inhibition and a greater level of exhibitionism than Americans are usually accustomed to. In short, you can visualize a situation in which you'd be willing to make a scene, "act out." Such behavior is antithetical to that encouraged in American culture. We are reminded of the manner in which several workshop participants have responded to strategies 6-19: "From the age of five, I was told 'Don't make a scene!' Now you're telling me that making a scene is precisely what I'm supposed to do. How can I reverse the habits of a lifetime?"

Choosing strategies 6-19 or maintaining a cluster of M's in that part of the scale also means that you can picture situations in which you would be willing to try to penetrate the rings of concentric circles (see chapter 5) in order to achieve your goal. You can accept that many Israelis will relate to you in terms of where you fit into the concentric circles in their lives. You can imagine situations in which the border between public and private or professional and personal will become less distinct.

The use of dramatic coping strategies also assumes that you're not willing to take no for an answer or that you accept that the no is negotiable.

If you've answered M to 22-26, you've indicated that you are willing to try out strategies which are directly confrontational, dramatic, and high profile, or you can visualize yourself becoming more comfortable with such strategies. Direct, high-profile confrontation in a business or bureaucratic setting receives little reinforcement in American culture.

In short, the greater the number of M's on items 6-26, the greater your flexibility. You are capable of visualizing situations in which your range of options will expand. This enhances the probability that you will adapt to Israeli culture.

Many Israelis, of course, are also comfortable with the low-key, reserved, nonconfrontational strategies at the top end of the scale. The range of their behavioral options, however, is broader than that of most Americans encountering Israeli culture for the first time. In new situations, or in familiar situations with new people, Israelis are likely to move from low-key strategies to concentric-circles penetration and more dramatic strategies at a faster pace. (Interestingly enough, this is also true when Israelis, themselves, are newcomers in the United States. Having been brought up in Israeli society, they have developed finely tuned antennae; they intuit which strategies, or combinations of strategies, are likely to result in the desired response in particular situations.)

If your response for items 27-30 was *N*, it means, of course, that you are opposed to the use or threat of force against property or individuals, *even if you think that it will prove effective*. In this respect, your responses are consistent with both American and Israeli middle-class cultural norms. If, in this exercise, you have compared your responses with those of members of your family or professional/social group, it is reasonable to assume that a consensus *N* existed around items 27-30.

If your *Y*'s clustered at the lower end of the numerical scale and your *N*'s began in the dramatic range and extended to the confrontational/aggressive end of the scale, your cultural adaptation will most likely be minimal. You will have to get along in Israel by using the behaviors with which you are already comfortable and/or by seeking out environments in which Israeli businesspeople or bureaucrats are accustomed themselves to adapting to *American* norms, expectations, and behavior patterns.

Summary

The above exercise has given you an opportunity to examine a menu of strategies for coping with commercial transactions and bureaucratic encounters. The "Coping-Strategy Menu" has also provided you with a chance to predict the direction and extent of your cultural adaptation to Israel. Of course, once you've predicted the maybes, you still have the opportunity to pick and choose. On any given day, the coping strategies you use will depend on any one, or perhaps several, of the following variables:

1. The level of stress you are willing to tolerate. Raising your voice (24), for example, may work, but it may make you feel so awful that it ruins your day. Returning twice to a given government office may prove less stressful than sticking around and negotiating past the first no.

2. Whom you are dealing with relative to gender, age, and position. An interaction with someone who reminds you of your mother may require a different set of coping strategies than one for dealing with a peer.

3. The situation: Observe what's happened to others who have gone before you. Did confrontation work? In what kind of mood is the clerk? What time of day is it? Is the official ready to leave for lunch?

A reminder: The issue is not whether one will adapt but where one will and where one won't. Try to be flexible and experimental, but recognize your limits. Do not attempt strategies that are clearly over the line. Your limits are legitimate, and if you are too uncomfortable, the strategy may well backfire.

Appendix B

Coping-Strategies Exercise
for the Workplace

Although we have used the menu approach as a model for coping and communicating in commercial and bureaucratic encounters, it can be applied in the workplace as well. Here's an example of a situation which calls for examination of a full range of coping strategies:

You are a design engineer at an American high-tech company. Your team has been working on a joint project with Israeli colleagues for eight months. You've been waiting for two months for a particular piece of documentation, or at least for a commitment as to when the documentation will be forthcoming. You've tried several times (E-mail and a telephone conversation) to get the Israelis to tell you what's going on and when you can expect the material. Every time you ask for this, Dov, your Israeli counterpart, says that he'll have it for you by the end of the week and, "Don't worry, John. It'll be OK."

You've been communicating with Dov, in the framework

of the project, for several months but have never met him face to face. From your limited contact, he seems like a pleasant person. And there's no question about the professional level of Dov and his team. They are excellent engineers, creative problem solvers. At this point, however, Dov's inability to understand the urgency of your request, together with his nonchalance, is beginning to get on your nerves.

You're stuck because you can't plan your work until you get the documentation from the Israelis.

Imagine yourself in the above situation. Then study the coping-strategy menu which begins below. It's been adapted for the workplace and differs from the menu in Appendix A.

The Coping-Strategy Menu for the Workplace

1. Withdraw—don't deal with the problem
2. Wait
3. Get someone else to deal with it
4. Ask questions to find out what the difficulty is
5. Straightforwardly explain your problem in a business-like manner
6. Show willingness to contribute to solution of the problem
7. Show willingness to compromise
8. Accept joint ownership of the problem
9. Validate the other person's priorities
10. Be extremely friendly
11. Appeal to the other person's sense of humor
12. Display empathy
13. Evoke sympathy for your plight
14. Play dumb

15. Exaggerate your situation

16. Evoke pity

17. Flatter

18. Flirt

19. Impose guilt

20. Continue repeating your request regardless of the other person's response

21. Refuse to leave/hang up until you get what you want

22. Raise your voice

23. Shout

24. Threaten to give him or her a bad reputation with colleagues

25. Threaten to report him or her to a higher authority, e.g., your boss

26. Threaten to report him or her to a higher authority, e.g., his or her boss

27. Bring the issue to your boss

28. Bring the issue to his/her boss

Study the menu. Now, do the following:

1. Place a Y (Yes) next to the coping strategies you feel comfortable with and/or use now as a visitor, prospective visitor, or someone in the U.S. engaged in ongoing contact with Israelis. (Or, if you have had no experience with Israelis, place a Y next to the coping strategies you feel comfortable with and/or use now in an *American* work setting.)

2. Place an M (Maybe) next to the coping strategies you might feel comfortable using three months from now. (Three months is long enough to form an impression of behavior patterns and gain some idea of how things work and what strategies are effective; yet it is too

short a period to understand the reasons for the behavior or to internalize unfamiliar norms.)

(If you are reading this chapter before your first
exposure to Israelis or your first visit to Israel, place an
M next to the coping strategies you *think* you would
feel comfortable using after three months.)

3. Place an N (No) next to the coping strategies you
believe you could not and would not ever use. These
are the strategies which you feel may compromise your
integrity. You may even find them morally abhorrent
or perhaps just repugnant or strongly uncharacteristic
of your personality.

4. Count and record the number of Y's, M's, and N's.
Look for clusters, e.g., groups of one answer in some
section of the menu.

5. Complete these sentences:
"Right now, I feel comfortable using strategies which
can be described as...":
Choose from the following list:
low-key
businesslike/professional
dramatic
confrontational
manipulative
nonconfrontational
other

"In three months (or three months after my arrival
in Israel), I may feel comfortable using strategies which
can be described as...":
Choose again from the above list.

Although the menu for the workplace differs from that in
Appendix A, the strategies fall into similar categories. Those
listed at the beginning of the numerical scale (lower numbers) are relatively low-key, straightforward, and nonconfrontational. The strategies in the middle range tend to be

more dramatic and personal. They call for adopting a less businesslike stance and may even be viewed as manipulative. The strategies listed at the end of the numerical scale (higher numbers) can be described as confrontational and/or aggressive. Numbers 22 and 23 are dramatically confrontational/ aggressive. Whoever employs them is willing to make a scene.

If you have a number of Y's at the beginning of the numerical scale (1-9) as well as at 20-21, your responses are consistent with both American and Israeli colleagues. When Americans and Israelis do this exercise, their cultural differences tend to appear in the middle and upper (higher numbers) range of the menu. Israelis seem to be comfortable with, and employ, a broader range of strategies in professional situations. If they have to deal with a situation identical to the one faced by the American design engineer (and they often do), Israelis will frequently choose dramatic strategies which personalize the issue as well as those that are straightforward and low-key or assertive and confrontational.

Israelis are willing to employ a broader range of coping strategies because the lines between behavior acceptable inside and outside of the workplace tend not to be as clearly drawn as they are for many Americans. What are the practical implications for your workplace interactions with Israelis? If you are an American for whom boundaries are clearly defined, you may decide not to make a special effort to broaden your range of coping strategies. On the other hand, in order to be more effective, you may choose to add one or two strategies from the menu to your repertoire. The challenge, of course, is to identify and adopt those strategies whose demands do not challenge your personal or professional integrity.

Bibliography

Adler, Nancy. *International Dimensions of Organizational Behavior*. Boston: Kent, 1986.

Bar-Tal, Daniel, and Dikla Antebi. "Siege Mentality in Israel," *International Journal of Intercultural Relations* 16, no.3 (1992): 251-75.

Benziman, Uzi. "Discovering America: Modern Times" (in Hebrew), *HaAretz*, 3 June 1984.

Elon, Amos. *The Israelis: Founders and Sons*, rev. ed. Jerusalem: Adam, 1981.

Gal, Reuven. *A Portrait of the Israeli Soldier*. New York: Greenwood Press, 1986.

Grossman, David. *Sleeping on a Wire: Conversations with Palestinians in Israel* (translated by Haim Watzman). New York: Farrar, Straus and Giroux, 1993.

Hattis Rolef, Susan, ed. *Political Dictionary of the State of Israel*. Jerusalem: Jerusalem Publishing, 1987, 1993.

Hazelton, Lesley. *Israeli Women: The Reality behind the Myths*. New York: Simon and Schuster, 1977.

Hofstede, Geert. *Culture's Consequences: International Differences in Work-Related Values*. Beverly Hills: Sage, 1980.

186

Katriel, Tamar. *Communal Webs: Communication and Culture in Contemporary Israel.* Albany: State University of New York Press, 1991.

————. *Talking Straight: Dugri Speech in Israeli Sabra Culture.* Cambridge: Cambridge University Press, 1986.

Rabinovitch, Danny. "Arabs in Jewish Neighborhoods" (in Hebrew), *HaAretz,* 13 August 1993.

Schoffman, Stuart. "Write It Again, Shmulik," *Jerusalem Report,* 9 April 1992.